SELECTED POEMS

Also by Douglas Stewart

POEMS
Green Lions
The White Cry
Elegy for an Airman
Sonnets to the Unknown Soldier
The Dosser in Springtime
Glencoe
Sun Orchids
The Birdsville Track
Rutherford
Collected Poems 1936–1967

VERSE PLAYS
The Fire on the Snow
The Golden Lover
Ned Kelly
Shipwreck
Fisher's Ghost

PROSE
The Flesh and the Spirit (Criticism)
A Girl with Red Hair (Short Stories)
The Seven Rivers (Reminiscences)
The Broad Stream (Criticism)
Norman Lindsay: A Personal Memoir (Biography)
Norman Lindsay's Cats
A Man of Sydney: An Appreciation of Kenneth Slessor (Criticism)
Writers of the Bulletin (Reminiscences)
Springtime in Taranaki (Reminiscences)

Douglas Stewart

SELECTED POEMS

Angus&Robertson
An imprint of HarperCollins*Publishers*

AN ANGUS & ROBERTSON BOOK
An imprint of HarperCollinsPublishers

First published in Australia in 1973
by Angus & Robertson Publishers
This edition published in 1992 by
CollinsAngus&Robertson Publishers Pty Limited (ACN 009 913 517)
A division of HarperCollinsPublishers (Australia) Pty Limited
25-31 Ryde Road, Pymble NSW 2073, Australia

HarperCollins Publishers (New Zealand) Limited
31 View Road, Glenfield, Auckland 10, New Zealand

HarperCollinsPublishers Limited
77-85 Fulham Palace Road, London W6 8JB, United Kingdom

National Library of Australia
Cataloguing-in-Publication data:

Stewart, Douglas, 1913–1985
    Selected poems
    ISBN 0 207 17614 0
    I. Title
A821.3

Cover details: Moon Over Ku-ring-gai by Margaret Coen
Courtesy of the artist
Printed in Australia by Griffin Press

10 9 8 7 6 5
96 95 94 93 92

FOREWORD

One reason why I am glad to have been asked to make this selection is that it has given me a chance to restore to life a minute poem called "Mosquito Orchid". I left it out of my *Collected Poems* in 1967 and it has been speaking to me ever since in a small plaintive subterranean voice, like a cricket.

The chief count I had against it was that the central image of this tiny orchid as a mosquito was not my own but was simply picked up from its popular name, which seemed too facile a way of making a poem. But then, while it was languishing in oblivion, it happened to be singled out for special approval by a critic I respected, which always does a poem a lot of good—for how can the author really know anything about it? And, on reflection, at least the "glinting and stinging" aspects of the image were mine, a genuine response to some needle-like intimations of the earth's vitality; and so was the carcass of the Christmas beetle, an object I had always been rather pleased to have added to the sum of English poetry. So, I realized, I was wrong to have been so cruel to "Mosquito Orchid"—I beg its pardon.

I might perhaps mention the other ways in which this selection differs from the *Collected Poems*, apart from the obvious fact that it is shorter.

It seemed to me convenient to group what remained of the poems from my first two books, *Green Lions* and *The White Cry*, under the heading "Early New Zealand Poems"; and it was tempting to place with those, as I have done, a few nostalgic poems about my native land written during my first two or three years in Sydney: chiefly the title poem from "Elegy for an Airman" (1940) and "The River" (which was originally entitled "The Waingongoro", only nobody in Australia could pronounce that) which made its appearance in book form as late as 1946 in *The Dosser in Springtime*—however I think it was written some years before that.

Apart from these and one or two other poems transferred into the New Zealand section I am afraid that *Elegy for an Airman* and the book that followed it, *Sonnets to the Unknown Soldier*, are very meagrely represented in this selection, as indeed, though a trifle more generously, they were in the *Collected Poems*. I hope that I have not again done an injustice. There are in fact a few poems I like in both these books but a selection has to be a selection and, as far as the longer poems are concerned, I find it now, in peacetime, very difficult to respond to the emotions we felt in the years of World War II.

One natural but disturbing result of omitting these wartime poems was, I discovered, that the selection then began to give the impression that the vast historical events of our time had made no impact on me at all: which was far from the truth. For this reason, among others, I have included a poem called "The Breaking Wave" which does mention that there were such things as bombers and submarines disturbing our peace of mind; and I note with some relief that "Elegy for an Airman" did at least clearly arise from the war if it didn't mention it, while, much later, "Rutherford" was to concern itself with the atomic bomb; but I suppose that on the whole my reaction to the violence of our time has been chiefly expressed, by image and implication, in the verse plays and *Glencoe*.

Partly for that reason, and partly because I do not think that in their merits and defects they can reasonably be separated from the rest of my poetry, I have included here extracts from each of the plays. *Glencoe*, which was originally intended to be a play but emerged of its own accord as a sequence of ballads, is included practically in full, except that I have left out my old friend Bottle-nosed Jock and one or two other pieces that seemed, for present purposes, dispensable. The effect, as in the omission (with others) of the opening and closing poems of "Worsley Enchanted", is to make both sequences a little more severe in their final effect than they were intended to be.

Finally, the selection is more up-to-date than either the *Collected Poems* or the small *Selected Poems* in the Australian Poets series. Most of the poems that were grouped under the title of "The Flowering Place" in the *Collected Poems* have here been assembled with other poems written since *Rutherford* was published, under the title "Later Poems".

D.S.

CONTENTS

vii

From SUN ORCHIDS

From RUTHERFORD

LATER POEMS

EARLY NEW ZEALAND POEMS

GREEN LIONS

The bay is gouged by the wind
In the jagged hollows green lions crouch,
And stretch,
And slouch,
And sudden with spurting manes and a glitter of haunches
Charge at the shore
And rend the sand and roar.

And inland, in offices and banks
Though trams clang down and heavy stone resists
The mutter of distant carnage still persists,
And men denied the jungle of young years

Grow taut, and clench their fists.

POPLAR IN THE MIMI VALLEY

The slate-blue snarl of storm is on the south
And northward looms Mount Messenger's surly bulk
But burning at the centre yellow and gold
The poplar towers and mocks the stunted growth
Of native trees to bony east and west
That have their thicker beauty but must sulk
To darker green when autumn and unrest
Warn them of rains and the tremendous cold.

She holds a golden coin between her teeth
This winter singer who is not afraid,
And wind or the dark audience of trees
Watching and envying, on the grass beneath,
Have showered tribute even as I do now,
Guinea on guinea, a golden cannonade;
And I have thought that milkers of the cow
In this harsh valley might rejoice as these.

3

Bronze tempest torrents over from the west
And gongs upon the eastern hill's nude bones,
And one sharp torch torments the skinny jungle
That to the gashed-out gully claws hard-pressed
So dark-grey green to greenish yellow glares.
All swirls, all like a driven water moans
Save that one tree that in the centre flares
And in all turmoil sings like golden shingle.

She holds a golden coin between her teeth,
And like a young girl in a darkened house
Showers the unasked rich plumage of her sap
To crafty eels in the thick creek beneath
And brutal earth and sour determined grasses.
And I have thought a milker of the cows
Who heavily through this surly valley passes
Might put a golden feather in his cap.

MENDING THE BRIDGE

Burnished with copper light, burnished,
The men are brutal: their bodies jut out square
Massive as rock in the lanterns' stormy glare
Against the devastation of the dark.
Now passionate, as if to gouge the stark
Quarry of baleful light still deeper there,
With slow gigantic chopping rhythm they hack,
Beat back and crumple up and spurn the black
Live night, the marsh-black sludgy air.

And clamour the colour of copper light
Swings from their hammering, and speeds, and breaks
Darkness to clots and spattering light, and flakes
Oily, like dazzling snow and storms of oil.
The night that never sleeps, quickens. The soil,
The stones and the grass are alive. The thrush awakes,
Huddles, and finds the leaves gone hard and cool.
The cows in the fields are awake, restless; the bull
Restless. The dogs. A young horse snorts and shakes.

4

Beneath the square of glaring light
The river still is muttering of flood,
The dark day when thick with ugly mud,
Swirling with logs and swollen beasts (and some
Still alive, drowning) it had come
Snarling, a foul beast chewing living cud,
And grappled with the bridge and tried to rend it,
So now these stronger brutes must sweat to mend it
Labouring in light like orange blood.

Men labour in the city so,
With naked fore-arms singed with copper light
And strangeness on them as with stone they fight,
Each meet for fear, and even the curt drill
Mysterious as trees and a dark hill.
But these are stronger, these oppose their might
To storm and flood and all the land's black power.
Burnished with sweat and lanterns now they tower
Monstrous against the marshes of the night.

THE GROWING STRANGENESS

I have a tree's tongue now and speak for stone
And cattle's bony moods I've made my own.
If difference is, it's one wry silver leaf
Or the faint spiral that the cricket shrills,
A valid phrase, but hardly qualifying
The blunt grey statement of New Zealand hills.

Yet while the blackbirds twittering their fear
At early owl or innocent brown hare
Sliver the huddled silver of the brushwood
And the dark hawk floats lonely and austere
Through coming night that rumbles on the farm
Like grey stones trundled through the watery air,

5

Aware of me, afraid, the browsing cattle
Lift heads and stare, alert for flight or battle
As if I were an alien bull advancing
Wary and dangerous through the evening cool;
As if that leaf's-breadth silver wryness made me
Stark and grotesque and massive as a bull.

Even in fields I love I am a stranger.
But beasts that sniffed and stiffened as for danger
Relax, and with their tongues, those rasping plumes,
Crop the pale grass and have no more alarm.
Who turns as I have turned to rove the fields
From glowing hearth, and talking, and the warm

Body of his beloved, will find me now,
If growing strangeness will his eyes allow,
Too less-than-human to disturb the cattle.
So has that first shrill quibble changed and grown,
Above the gully, set on the grey hill
Impersonal, impersonal I am as strange and lone

As a dead tree, a pillar of black stone.

HOSTILE MOUNTAIN

Here is the patient hostility of rock
And water calls with a cold voice, like iron
That drops with a hushed clang down glooms of ice.
Old stone is angry, the dead volcano
Holds something of stubborn hatred even yet;
Or why do men who have climbed the sour ridges
Feel such a need for gossip on returning,
Such desperate need for the warmth of human words;
Why do the fools with kodaks hang back from the canyons,
Afraid that invisible hands will push them over?

6

Here wind is assassin, but greater evil
Lies in wait beneath the slopes that glisten;
Or why do the girls who sport amongst the snow
Suddenly pause . . . and listen . . .
And men on the ski-ground shout falsely loud, and laugh

With a hollow sound the crags toss to and fro?

MORNING

Move brownly now, and with a leafy rustle
Like earth's limbs slackening as sun grows warm;
Lie still, or edging to me, move as slightly
As if slow sap had snaked along your form.
A sound like twittering sticks proclaims the darling
Irresponsible joyance of the starling
That now with ecstacy, with spiralling silver,
Makes shrill the sunlight's thick bee-golden swarm.

Move brownly now, acknowledge these wild matins
As stone-blue gums would do, with only a sweet
Tremor like bells in your slow secret veins.
Your lightest move, your stillness is as fleet
As trout in the far pools, as slender gums
That chafe for speed, and when a young wind comes
Jingle and stamp, and delicately stampede
Like silver deer through blue-leaved groves of heat.

The minutes brush like leaves; I dare not breathe
Lest that faint storm disturb them as they pass.
Drowse, and I'll tell you of birds like small green leaves
Pecking the yellow peaches in the grass,
The wax-eyes with their sorrowful thin cry
A leaf might make if it had will to try.
Drowse, and I'll bring you hills, and small birds trilling
Like water in a thin green reed of glass.

Move brownly now, and with a leafy rustle
Like earth's limbs slackening towards the heat.
I find in you in this warm flowering hour
That makes the night's dark loveliness complete
Not sleep, but more than sleep, a crystal dream,
A magpie like a bell in a clear stream;
Not peace, but more than peace; the noise of trees
Larks, and the auburn sibilance of wheat;

So drowse my dear with your brown leafy rustle,
While birds and bells and water keep you sweet.

CROWD

Each of this salt and sullen mass has once
Felt suddenly, desperately individual,
And mad to lose that loneliness has plunged
Back to the sea, at smothering flesh has plunged
With a hot mouth, with a wild call.
Each of these has once been singled out
As one miraculous, a million suns,
Green jewels and rubies, more strange than words could speak,
And so adored, has answered sick with doubt,
"I know you not; and I am not unique.
I am no different at all."

So now, a single mass, the rank dank waves
Roar from the hollow building, and divide
In two dark swirls, and merge, and onward surge,
And roaring come, and split, and onward surge,
A headlong ocean, a blind tide.
Standing defiant, the rock on which it shatters,
I remember: each has been called more strange than mountains,
Each is alone and each must die, must die:
Each of that sea where the traffic screams and clatters
Must fight his fellows, or follow, or stand as I
Stockstill, and grinning with a hard pride.

8

SHINBONE AND MOSS

To extricate the river from the willows,
One golden with the loot of ravaged farms
One autumn-auburned flowing through the winter
Compels me like a trumpet-call to arms;
But both are locked with stones and moss and fern,
Congealed in stubborn silence with their fellows
No word can burn
No wind or wave or eyes' white wedge can splinter.

Here reaches only half the lone cold sun
With flickered greens and indecisive yellows.

Plainer it is! Upon a cold white hone,
A cold white bone green moss is feeding on,
Sharpens the greenlight, focuses the gloss.
Here at the tree's root, dead a long age gone,
Shinbone is white and weather-chewed and dank,
And so much like, and both so like a stone
Is my own shank
I clutch my flesh to feel if it be moss.

And here's the truth of that bleak sharpened sun:
One day I'll be no more than that green bone.

All day has stone pushed up through flat and hill
And sky pushed down with pressure of hard slate,
And the tombed skylark stabbing song's white wedges
Could only groove and grieve, not penetrate.
On sapless grass a foiled and sandstone colour,
Lack-lustre sheep were more than sandstone-still
Than dead grass duller,
And dead and greenstone-heavy were the hedges.

Now by the river half the lone cold sun
Makes fitfuller dumb rock and river's will.

9

Here gold-beard sun may drink and half atone
For tree and stream thus knotted in dark doubt,
But the gnawed bone will green and moulder on,
And in the pools the cool mysterious trout
Like moving stones will move amongst the stones.
Less sure than water of the uncertain sun
Darkly my bones
Chill vegetable lips will feed upon

Now make their peace, now triumph and acknowledge
The cold, sweet company of moss and stone.

WATCHING THE MILKING

I

In the ashen evening a bird's song spouts in silver
That swirls to the shed where an engine spits and chugs.
The yard is muddy. Sunk to the knees the cows
Await the sucking cup, the hand that tugs,
Content and chewing, and not afraid of man
Or the weird machine that robs their swollen dugs.

2

As torchlight stabs a pool and splits the stillness
The madness of motherhood tore these gentle eyes;
And the fawn cows that stand so quietly in the yard
Felt tides of ancient passion in them rise,
And knew great tenderness, were wild and savage,
And bawled in torment to the lost calf's cries.

3

"They soon forget . . . This happens every year."
The light fades, and the thrush no longer sings.
"And every year, and every year, and always."
A match glows. The odour of warm milk brings
Remembrance of hay, and woodsmoke, and horses; and then
Of pine-trees and scented hair, and magical things.

The hills grow dark, are monstrous upon the earth—
Where leads the trail beyond their sprawling weight?
Day is a broken dream, and night fantastic;
Ghost in a ghostly world alone and late,
I might have been watching the cold craters of the moon,
Or Pithecanthrope gesturing to his mate.

HEART OF THE WORLD

I feel now like some mariner who lies
Too tired for sleep upon his narrow bed,
While overhead
The stars are crackling in the glimmering skies,
And sea beneath is ebony fired with green.
While so he lies, so utterly serene,
He hears the engines beat,
Thud and repeat,
In perfect rhythm, in lovely shuddering time.
Their steady rhyme
Seems far below him, far away
In some vast chasm . . . a great machine
Throbbing and throbbing, far away.

And so upon your warm white breast I lie
In utter peace, in rich abandonment.
O heart content!
There is no terror in the sputtering sky
Nor in the oily bay that's stabbed with green.
Now while I lie, your heart beats quick and keen;
I hear it darkly pound,
Thud and resound,
In perfect rhythm, in lovely shuddering time.
Its steady rhyme
Seems far below me, far away
In reeling space . . . a great machine
Throbbing and throbbing, far away.

MOMENT

The black cup of a winter dusk
though sullen with the late eclipse
of baleful wailing yellow light
on sodden field and tree's gnawed husk
suddenly shrivelled up my lips.

A white bell with a yellow tongue
across my mind's dark ocean swung
as shining as a choir of dew.

Then a belated blackbird flew
shrieking as though a madman laughed,
but had no power to break the spell
of lily chimes and holy bell
that on my mind's dark ocean rocked
shocked by that black and furious draught.

TABLET FOR THE LONELY WATER

Suppose the shifting white fire of her feet
Branded the pale drowned stones with deathless grooves
As birds' feet sand, as hares print frosted grass,
As deer in flight cut snowfields with the fleet
Delicate sharp diamonds of their hooves,
Her footprints so on stones, those dim flat moons,
Through fleeting flutes would gleam or stiller glass
For eels to writhe upon and water slither
Till all stones rot and all streams dry and wither.
But that would not avail, not carven stones,
Over those moon-strange far configurations
Whio would sail, the lone blue mountain-drake,
And whistle his cold mate, as blind to wonder
As his dark kin that torrenting to their lake
Care not a feather's ruffle for clanging on
The meaningless contortions of the moon.

No, that would not avail. And if a boy
Exploring the warm secrets of the hills
Chanced on this lonely water, saw the carving,
The rune of all our splendour, all our joy
So burned in stone where water chimes and trills
Would be but idle fancy, such a tale
To make his elders ache their sides with laughing,
And to himself the footprints' milky blaze
Only a moment's Crusoe-like amaze.
No that would not avail, would not avail,
No man would follow him, no, no man come,
Conceive her reeling beauty and bow down.
Though her white feet were written into rock
They were but bones in a sea-eaten town,
The script but the pale record of a ghost
Between a brown hill and a blue hill lost.

The stream has nothing in it to remember
What naked feet or bodies made it holy;
Not mint nor sedge nor golden isle of gorse
Nor little crayfish scuttling through the amber
Nor eel in browner hollows writhing slowly
Can speak her fire that should have chiselled stone,
So I must grave her image in still verse
To gleam like snow and marble through a time
When iron days all else may overcome.
This tablet will remain though she be gone
And stream go too, past the last spur's blue shoulder
And wind into the hills beyond all finding,
And those cool eddies that caressed her feet
Be utterly lost in winding and unwinding
Of the lost listless tides hauled creaking on
Cordage of silver, the windlass of the moon.

ON THE CREST OF THE RIDGE

So much of shade and silver, ridge and valley,
Dark bass of fern and far-off treble of rills,
So much of charred hard wood and breeze-tongued grass
And all this moon-furred jungledom of hills
As you can see before you, O my love,
Take break for brutes or flutes as passion wills.
In silver anguish chained too fierce to move
I say take break or spurn, but do not turn
Where down behind you, scarred with years and fern,
Lit with a blacker magic than the moon's
Lies half the ridge and half my life in shade.

Light-years of hills lie clear and still before you,
The gullies fleeced with peace and dewed with light.
Take, break, or make to violins
Crying the silver agony of night,
So much of shade and silver, crest and glade,
Sheep-sad hollow or blade-glad height
As you can see before you ere they fade.
My lips, my limbs are here, but O forbear
Backwards, my love, from this keen crest to stare
At half the ridge and half my life in shade,
Lit with a blacker magic than the moon's.

TURN EAGLE, LARK

O singing heart turn hawk; turn eagle, lark:
The air is cold, the dawn strains from night

And time's gaunt landscape shambles up from dark
To lie like iron in the harsh white light.

Be far, dark-winged dark-blooded bird be far
With windy sweep towards the last sharp star

Over the wilderness of years and over
The marshes conquered, peaks for climbing soon,

And far and near and as far as flight can cover,
A landscape crazed and monstrous as the moon.

Veer down my bird of prey, veer down to mark
One flickering campfire braving out the dark

And in the convulsive stillness of the ranges
Bloodshed and shouting by its lonely light

From travellers lost in time and mad with fright.
No roads are here, the landscape never changes:

Turned eagle now, my dark bird veer and climb,
And solitary and cruel range over time.

HAYSTACK

The creamy frost of toi-toi plumes
Above the rushes' blue-green shrilling
Forewarns the farm that winter comes,
But the rich land is not unwilling,

For where begins the yellow sward
Against that trembling sea-green rumour,
Strong hands have here in haystack stored
A whole green field, a whole gold summer.

The field is bare that once concealed
So much of little fur and feather,
Too shorn of cover now to shield
A fieldmouse from the hawk or weather;

And as on yellow pools at eve
The silver rains of insects bubble,
Bright showers of starlings pelt and grieve
The still and saffron lake of stubble.

Yet what was there is gathered up
And will not perish for the cold:
Though all the suns of buttercup
Went down in one wild dusk of gold,

And daisy-moons like snow were shed
On soft green oceans toppling over,
And lark and hare in terror fled
The crumpling purple flames of clover,

The meadow in the memoried stack
Is gathered safe for winter food.
Already now the rains turn black
The walls of hay, the thatchlike hood,

And I beside the cold, shrill marsh
Rejoice I heard that bitter rumour,
And stacked me here for time grown harsh
A whole green field, a whole gold summer.

THE WHITE CRY

Where boughs green not with leaves but moss
Cathedral-cold enclosed the wry
Vines struggling through a world of loss
And trees' growth heavier than a sigh,
I saw the youngest lamb in the world
Beside the oldest tree in the wood.
Its delicate fleece with twilight pearled,
In white astonishment it stood,
The only light in that green gloom,
The only warmth in bleak July.
So small against the dusk and doom
To which the tree through greenlight's sigh
Strode onwards with a vast slow tread,
So frail against the breath of ice

(Though on white snow its red blood bled
To make a winter sacrifice)
It had no power to shake the wood,
That could not hurt a blade of grass.
I saw it stricken as it stood
For lumbering centuries to pass:
Against the tree's dark vastitude
A dream, a white cry, meaningless,
Though it were nailed on that huge rood.

LOOK NOW FOR COUNTRY ATLAS

Soft weight of russet light
On field, on woodland sleeping
For all its dusk tells clearer
Than noon's blue bushfire leaping
Elate among the trees
What heavy load, what shadow
The land's true being is.

Now quenched with dew, with truth,
The trees my dream's blue flame
Had burned to pillared silver
Move to the night, proclaim
Allegiance dark and fast
With the brute earth that under
The auburn dusk grows vast.

Look now for country Atlas:
Lightly enough he bears
Who moves among dark trees
His world of simple cares,
The wood to warm him by,
The paddock thick with grass,
The stack not built; but I,

True load not shouldered yet
And nowhere here to find,
Feel the red-brown light a burden
Lowering on my mind,
And walk with heavy tread
Homeward from farm and Atlas
To glass and book and bed.

VILLAGE

Mooning here and hungering after
Darker hearts and whiter laughter,
Straws of these in this village
I clutch at or must drown in rage—
This man's lechery that man's greed
River and wood and sluttish Nan
Sulking her body out to trade—

But town seems half preposterous,
A story told in public-house,
And sot or cricketer, stream or wood,
Nan's sulky eyes and smouldering blood,
Have only for my wandering gaze
Fantastic charm and homesickness
Like memories of childhood days.

PERCEIVED IN CHILL AND WINDY DUSK

Perceived in chill and windy dusk
Night's dark demand of tears and blood,
And still the ghost assumes my form
To freeze the heat of body's mood.
Too calm for touch or terror still,
Aloof and cool as streams at night,
He stands within my body's frame
With flesh of cold and yellow light;
As once he stood when two were parted,
A pillar of cold yellow light
Unmoved through silver storms of tears
And blood and anguish in the night;
As he will stand within my flesh
In sun or storm, in calm or flood,
To still with chill and yellow light
Life's dark demand of tears and blood.

AS THE MOON'S HAND

When day breaks white a song fades whiter,
Her song like snowy silver water
That love's deft hand made sigh and flash
All night from her white lyre of flesh,
As the moon's hand on water wrings
Song from its creamy rippling strings.

O whiten poem for her sake
Whose whiteness locks the note I seek,
That you may tell when day grows hard
What creamy fire of song I heard,
What dream of snow and silver broke
When moon was lost and birds awoke.

THE GRASSES BEND WITH FROST

The grasses bend with frost,
The silver grasses bend;
It has been good here talking
And now, goodnight my friend.

Bowed, so bound to-night—
And now the black pines show
The mountain towering white,
The paddocks white below.

Fade down the pathway, ghost:
And seasons ago she went.
But mind still, bound and lost,
At the dark gate is bent
In manacles of frost.

HERITAGE

All this too-savage grace
Of life like snow on rock
And music ringing black
From the rowan-bleeding burn
Speaks now as speaks my face
Of a dead man's return.

Past me and past my father
And before his father's time
Some young man bore my name
And wore my face and form
And found among the heather
As I in my time—storm.

O my dead comrade, my master,
Jolting my hands to their work
Rocking my heart in the dark
Staring at life from my eyes,
When will you yield to disaster,
When will you sleep and be wise?

O my dead kinsman, my friend,
Whose voice is harsh in my throat,
What struggle not fought out
On Appin moor and hill,
And never perhaps to end,
Torments our wild blood still?

Where the red rowan glittered
Over the burn's dark thunder,
What sucked your spirit under
And flung it up, oh, hurled
Its pride and rage to be shattered
On the black rocks of the world?

I would endure for you
Whom I love as my own brother
All the soul's thunderous weather;
I would turn my flesh to stone
To see the long winter through
For you, for men, for my son:

But the spring is slow in coming
And you—and I, possessed—
Like mountains and thunder best.
O my proud ghost, my master,
Be in my bloodstream drumming
The joy of our disaster,

For I have no heart but yours.
It is your dead hand that touches
Hand and hair, and clutches
Torrent and rock and tree;
It is only your faith endures
And lives my life for me.

ELEGY FOR AN AIRMAN

In memory of Desmond Carter, a Pilot Officer of the R.A.F.,
killed in action 1939.

Only the trees were dark behind trees in the bush
And only the blackberries stained our mouths like blood;
The thrush like a fountain sang in the heart of the willows
And our shadows moved with the trout in the sunny water;
And we were the hares and the deer, we lived in a wood
Where keepers were big and notices said "No Shooting".

We lived in a castle, too, we were knights and princes
Some day or never to ride from our castle of fire
That sprang from the black roots dug from the Ngaere swamp
And shut us away in a tower of flame from the winter
When the pine-trees howled to each other like dogs and women
And the hooves of the rain struck their icy sparks from the roof.

We lived in a mirror, too, where our faces were marble,
While the seasons rolled like cumulus, white and remote.
Sometimes the eyes were troubled: incredible murder,
Bankruptcy, fire, a train and a car at a crossing;
But the storm passed over, the glass was clear in a week
And all of us lived for ever and were happy.

The boy was the heart of it all, was the hare and the eel,
Knew the weasel's way to the thrush's nest in the boxthorn;
The boy was the prince whose armour shone by the fire,
And the crystal core of the mirror, the light in the eyes.
Now the boy is dead and no one will play in the woods
Or kill the giants and marry the golden princess.

When death was a blackbird cold by the muddy roadside
And grief was a game of burial played in the garden,
A word was a thing you could hold, like a toy or a pet.
Hate was as simple as winter beating the window,
Tall neighbours walked like pine-trees with nothing to hide,
And God was behind the altar on Sunday mornings.

The signpost was plainly a madman, a wooden drunkard,
Babbling of places that lived in his moon of a mind,
For east was the mushroom field and west were the blackberries,
And north or south the train disappeared in a swamp
Or butted its head on the blue stone walls of the distance
Beyond which were bears and tigers, or maybe nothing.

A mother ran in a dream with her black hair streaming
And hacked the signpost down and broke its arms,
But it stood again in the morning, wooden and hostile,
And said that the dogs and cats had a track through the hedge
And the road was white in frost and steel in rain
And the blue stone walls would crumble away at a touch.

The road was white in the morning and breathing was silver
And the red hare leapt to her death from the rushes at Mata
And the snapper bucked on the line off Rapanui,
And the boy began to die with the beast and fish,
To die with the wild duck shot on the lonely river
And the trains that thundered to cities and iron harbours.

This was my friend who died with me out of boyhood,
Was young with me, and hungered for strife and triumph,
And chose the brilliance of flight to complete the pattern
Of speed and light he had learned from our mountain streams.
O my friend who have taken this other death alone,
The castle was always a dream, but you lived like a king.

I could wish that in death you had staked the claim of your dust
In our land that is ruled by neither the dead nor the living
But the wind and the bracken waving on masterless hills
And the surf like an avalanche whitening the Mokau coastline.
But, living, you gave us your mirth and the strength of your limbs,
And your laughter is fresh on the rivers, your strength on the fields.

No one should die and not be wept by women,
For death is no blackbird buried to feed the sunflowers
But the empty room and the clothes to give to the neighbours
And the fairy tale proved to be folly, the mirror broken,
And the fire not lit because nothing can warm the heart.
The women have wept for you, comrade. But I who remember

The childhood as far off as China, the road white with frost,
The rush of the hare and the boar at bay in the gorge,
The wind on the ice and the girls like burning snow,
The roar of the train and the rusty shriek of the harbour,
And the way we coughed and laughed in a London fog,
Remember the way of a man, that you sang and were strong.

Always beyond the roof that fingers could reach
Was life like a blue day, not to be held in the hand;
And caught in its day your silver statement of laughter
Is a fountain they cannot bury under the clay.
O my friend, your life goes echoing on through time
As the thrush still rings in the mind when the willows darken.

THE RIVER

God knows where the wild duck wintered, on what cold lake
While the mist was still in the raupo she heard the guns,
Rose, circled and was gone with the lucky ones
To some remoter peace no man could break;
God knows what months of terror or delight she spent
While our willows were bare and our paddocks under the frost
And vast over Egmont the snow spread its glistening tent,
The stream running cold all the way from mountain to coast;

But spring after spring when the willow put forth again
Its joy in the yellow buds and the green of the leaf,
She came again to the same rough nest on the cliff—
Bound to that place by what most lovely chain!
Held like the tree, held like myself, I know,
In the frozen season and most of all in the sweet
To that one place where the torrent of melted snow
Flashed to her breast and sang on the stones at her feet.

Bound to that place by what mysterious love!
O shining and winding water, winding in me
And moving towards a song, as in the tree
To bud and leaf the sap's cool currents move,
Never have I lost, no never at any time
However ice-bound, never in any place
However distant, one eddy's splash or chime,
One ripple's flash, one still pool's darker grace.

Passion and disaster, knowledge of love and hate,
Battle of mind and body against the world
Where the rivers of men and traffic roared and swirled,
The lonely rage of the spirit wrestling with fate:
So much went into the making of a man.
But always under the struggle, oh deep below,
The grey stones stood, and one clear river ran
And into the sea of a life brought down the snow.

Into the man's mind, yes, the boy's unfurls
In rings of water and light where the kingfisher dives
To eel and crayfish living their shadowy lives
By rocks that waver as the current glides and swirls;
And the boy's mind comes with a sparkle of sun and the shock
On the swimmer's limbs, till the body is free and flowing
And flesh and mind and spirit like the wavering rock
Are one with the river, going where the water is going.

How often, too, in fantasy or in dream,
Turned country man, or painter of earth and cloud,
My days have sung as they passed, far from the crowd,
Following from sea to snow this restless gleam:
The sombre pools; the light in a sky of willows;
The red and weedy roots where the eddy is dark
And the dead leaf spins and yellows; the stony shallows
Where the silver flames of the rapids flicker and spark;

25

The shingle bank where the gaunt old crusher stood
And the big trout hid in the run or leaped and splashed
When the stoneflies danced and the sunset colours flashed;
The broken pillars of Chiselhurst's ancient wood,
The haunted hollows where the sunlight came to dance
Like a girl in a ruined temple: by twist and turn,
By reach and run and banks where the mosses glance,
Mile after mile till the snow lay white on the fern.

But deeper than this, deeper than boyish play;
Beyond all this, daydream or dream's delight,
That sombre water burns like stars in my night,
That silver water trembles like wings in my day;
That song of water, like women crying or singing,
Rings in my depths where still is all sound and strife;
That living water, chill from the ice, or bringing
All summer's richness, runs at the roots of my life.

As if I had built my life like some clamorous town
Where crowds jostle and voices shout in confusion
And traffic howls—phantoms at war in illusion!—
While under it all, the joy and the thunder, deep down
The hidden river pursues its own calm course:
Known to be there, some river-mist always known,
But only at the bitterest crisis of rage or remorse
Or the flowering of love—listen! Water on stone.

At the end of a life illusion falls away.
When the city falls, oh then in that last day, river,
I shall come back to you as a man to his lover,
As the bird comes back when her wild blood sets the day
And the first leaf breaks on the willow. Symbol or truth,
Let the day disclose! But a man's what his spirit knows;
And what I have known for truth, now as in youth,
Is one clear river, coming down cold from the snows.

THE CRICKET

I can't get over it,
I pipe and I trill, said the cricket;
And if you should ask me why
A full-grown insect should sit
In a tiny tunnel in the ground
And make a piping sound,
I really have no reply;
I can't get over it.

What is my song about?
I leave it to you, said the cricket.
I know that the elders will die
But most of the eggs hatch out;
I know the roots of the grass
And perils that thump as they pass;
I like to announce I am I,
And that's what my song's about.

If you come clumping by
I quake and am still, said the cricket.
There are bandicoots, cats and boys
And frightening creatures that fly,
And under my log or my stone
I prefer to be left alone,
Resuming my piping noise
As soon as you're safely by.

I'd sooner never be heard
On the whole, I think, said the cricket.
My love who has faultless taste
Opines I can pipe like a bird;
And, dank and thorny and brown,
I trill when the sun goes down
And none of it goes to waste
As long as my love has heard.

Say what you darn well like,
It's not a bad song, said the cricket.
Here while the grassblades glisten
Thrusting each frosty spike
From the earth where we serve our term
With the blind grub and the worm,
I shrill and the tall stars listen,
Say what you darn well like.

THE BUNYIP

The water down the rocky wall
Lets fall its shining stair;
The bunyip in the deep green pool
Looks up it to the air.

The kookaburra drank, he says, then shrieked at me with laughter,
I dragged him down in a hairy hand and ate his thighbones after;
My head is bruised with the falling foam, the water blinds my eye
Yet I will climb that waterfall and walk upon the sky.

The turpentine and stringybark,
The dark red bloodwoods lean
And drop their shadows in the pool
With blue sky in between.

A beast am I, the bunyip says, my voice a drowning cow's,
Yet am I not a singing bird among these waving boughs?
I raise my black and dripping head, I cry a bubbling cry,
For I shall climb the trunks of trees to walk upon the sky.

Gold and red the gum-trees glow,
Yellow gleam the ferns;
The bunyip in the crimson pool
Believes the water burns.

I know the roots of rocks, he says, I know the door of hell;
I ate the black man's daughter once, I know my faults full well;
Yet sunset walks between the trees and sucks the water dry,
And when the whole world's burnt away I'll walk upon the sky.

The little frogs they call like bells,
The bunyip swims alone;
Across the pool the stars are laid
Like stone by silver stone.

What did I do before I was born, the bunyip asks the night;
I looked at myself in the water's glass and I nearly died of fright;
Condemned to haunt a pool in the bush while a thousand years
    go by—
Yet I walk on the stars like stepping-stones and I'll climb them
    into the sky.

A lady walks across the night
And sees that mirror there;
Oh, is it for herself alone
The moon lets down her hair?

The yabbie's back is green for her, his claws are opal-blue,
Look for my soul, the bunyip says, for it was a jewel too.
I bellowed with woe to the yabbie once, but all I said was a lie,
For I'll catch the moon by her silver hair and dance her around the
    sky.

LADY FEEDING THE CATS

I

Shuffling along in her broken shoes from the slums,
A blue-eyed lady showing the weather's stain,
Her long dress green and black like a pine in the rain,
Her bonnet much bedraggled, daily she comes
Uphill past the Moreton Bays and the smoky gums
With a sack of bones on her back and a song in her brain
To feed those outlaws prowling about the Domain,
Those furtive she-cats and those villainous toms.

31

Proudly they step to meet her, they march together
With an arching of backs and a waving of plumy tails
And smiles that swear they never would harm a feather.
They rub at her legs for the bounty that never fails,
> They think she is a princess out of a tower,
> And so she is, she is trembling with love and power.

2

Meat, it is true, is meat, and demands attention
But this is the sweetest moment that they know
Whose courtship even is a hiss, a howl and a blow.
At so much kindness passing their comprehension
—Beggars and rogues who never deserved this pension—
Some recollection of old punctilio
Dawns in their eyes, and as she moves to go
They turn their battered heads in condescension.

She smiles and walks back lightly to the slums.
If she has fed their bodies, they have fed
More than the body in her; they purr like drums,
Their tails are banners and fountains inside her head.
> The times are hard for exiled aristocrats,
> But gracious and sweet it is to be queen of the cats.

THE LIZARDS

My wife is a lovely leathery green, the blue-tongued lizard said;
Her eyes are as red as bulldog ants, lurking in holes in her head;
Her body is made of the speckled grass, a violet grows on her tongue,
And I could watch her for fifty years if nobody blundered along.

The broken ridge like a bullock's ribs lies crumbling under the blue,
But the granite skull will last my time, and there's room for my truelove, too;
If I were a lizard half my size and out for a girl or a walk,
I think I'd be taking another track, and I wouldn't stop to talk.

32

Down in the valley the river shines, the willows waver and gleam,
And maybe it's you the plovers mean when they open their beaks
    and scream.
If I were as young and green as you, I'd take no risks, my boy—
Why not go off and drown yourself in the glimmering Duckmaloi?

Over the valley the gum-trees grow, the vast blue ranges loom,
The world is crowded with wives to steal and the world is full of
    room.
If I had hissed and glared like you I'd feel that I'd done enough—
Why don't you climb Mount Bindo there and see if you can't fall
    off?

If I opened my jaws myself like that, the blue-tongued lizard said,
And then if they closed again like this they'd just about fit your
    head;
There's a certain pain in having to fight but there's also a certain
    joy,
And the more you bite my belly or leg the more you'll pay, my boy.

I lay on my rock with the sun on my back and nothing but love
    in my soul,
But if I am forced to gasp and claw and roll and fight in a hole,
If I am forced to fight in the dirt under the blue of the sky
—The black snake lives in the briar-bush and he will be kinder
    than I.

Waddle away with a wounded air, the blue-tongued lizard said,
The ant and the crow will nurse you well and tuck you safely in
    bed.
We were at peace, my wife and I, before you blundered along,
And now she will soothe my scaly side with her beautiful purple
    tongue.

33

THE BREAKING WAVE

Winter on earth, and the sea looming like winter,
Storming the forts of the hard Australian coast;
And nowhere peace, unless in the breaking wave
—Snow on the rocks and the sky jagged with frost—

The heart can sustain its load, like a hush of foam,
One moment of exaltation. Too much like the roar
Of guns in the heavy whiteness, too like the gunfire
That shakes our world to pieces, the surf on this shore

Explodes and crashes and stuns, for a man to dream
That peace like a rock-pool, the sunken pillar of light
Eternal under the breakers, will glitter again
Ice-blue with the turn of the water, today or tonight.

Who will take his stand on the cliff with the broom and tea-tree,
Stubborn and bent, like sheep with their backs to the weather,
Will not today or tomorrow sing you that song
"My girl and I lay down in the sky together";

But will sing with the iron surf of mine and torpedo,
Shipwreck and death by drowning, the droning bomber;
Of a sky like sea and man like a shark beneath it,
And winter too strong to sit and dream of summer.

And who will go down to the beach to pick up shells
In the boom of the surf, let him clench them tight in his hand,
Say "Here was a pretty thing!—was love, was laughter;
Such things have been known to exist, even on land."

OLD IRON

There are no instructions here for that dazzling man,
So frail in front of the engine, who one fine day
Will leap to the track and switch the points, they say,
And save the time from disaster, set the great wheels
Roaring at last on the true, the only way:

34

No more than a lump of iron for that man to look at
As I am looking while the crabs scuttle and hide
And the backs of the limpets dry as the seaweed has dried
To the stillness of stone, and the wrack cast up by the sea
Rusts in the sun and awaits the returning tide.

One of those weathered and very mad old men
Who live alone in their humpies, outlaws alike
From the holiday crowds who snatch at the waves and shriek
Like gulls at a shoal, and whatever goal or disaster
Or mere receding distance our time will strike,

One of those withered and very mad old men
Concerned with their own slow rusting in natural leisure
Should be here with me, is here in my mind to treasure
This twisted bit of a ship, this battered junk,
And stretch his hand to the iron with a cry of pleasure,

Though nobody else, unless some wandering boy,
Is likely to spare it a glance. If a dumb yearning
Calls iron, after the hammering and the burning,
Back to its native earth, this has its wish:
Seabird and fish accept it as rock returning,

And as flesh and bone of the earth it takes the sun
And glows with life, or receives the sea and crumbles.
And now as always when the mind's old madman stumbles
On some such rock, and pauses, and fills with light
At an apparition of Earth, his hand trembles

And stretches out to the simple touch of the iron
As towards another hand, or to warm spring air,
Water or tree or stone, in a gesture of prayer
And sweet communion with things that accept in peace
The rhythms of earth beyond our control or care.

Lava on Egmont, shellrock at Mangamingi,
There were always sacred rocks and sacred trees,
And beside the breakwater cutting the violent seas
At far New Plymouth like a searchlight thrust in a storm,
A gigantic rusty anchor took its ease;

And far away back into childhood at Opunake
Was a shaft of iron in a rock, so deeply thrust
No giant could shake it though spray had flaked it with rust;
And no one could tell us why it was driven there
By the old mysterious men, themselves now dust.

What shall we say, old madman, of this old iron,
Meteorite on a lonely Australian reef
From the age's whirling planet of hope and grief?
Iron that stands like the earth's accusing ghost
In city buildings, iron that without relief

Roars on the rails of the world, both track and engine
For the whole adventure and drive of the urgent mind,
Lies calmly here, forgetting tormented mankind
In the older life of the earth where the simple creatures
Obey their natures and the rock is dumb and blind.

And likely enough, one of those mad old men
Will creep from his hole when the age has crashed at last
And stare at the wreck of iron and mutter aghast
"So the blind rush came to this; the earth has got them."
But the old man hides in a hole; we thunder past,

Committed to high adventure, and what we have seen,
Who cannot see our far-off stopping place,
Of the life of the earth growing or crumbling in grace
Is half a meeting in joy and half a good-bye,
Like seeing in the rain at night a woman's face.

BILL POSTERS

You won't get pity, you won't get pardon,
They'll search the cellar, they'll probe the garden,
Bill Posters, O Bill Posters.
It's no good saying you never did it,
They'll find that body wherever you hid it:
Murder is nice but the laws forbid it,
Bill Posters will be prosecuted.

While you lay asleep by the side of your wife
Somebody saw you sharpen the knife,
Bill Posters, O Bill Posters.
Somebody owned the sack you stole,
Somebody saw you digging the hole,
Somebody knows he'll have your soul,
Bill Posters will be prosecuted.

You shall be charged with breaking the peace,
Banged and badgered by large police,
Bill Posters, O Bill Posters.
They'll come with summons, they'll come with injunction,
They'll come with handcuffs and no compunction,
The law is firm and the law will function,
Bill Posters will be prosecuted.

Under the bed or behind the door,
They want that man who started the war,
Bill Posters, O Bill Posters.
On village and city crashes the bomb,
They shriek at the sky where the bomb came from
And your heart cries out like a voice from the tomb
Bill Posters will be prosecuted.

High is the mountain, wide is the plain,
You'll never escape that voice in your brain,
Bill Posters, O Bill Posters.
Dive in the surf, hit a ball about,
Hide in the film when the lights go out,
You'll still be hearing the newsboys shout
Bill Posters will be prosecuted.

Body of infant found in gutter,
Down in the slums you have heard them mutter,
Bill Posters, O Bill Posters.
The old mare's bolting and you can't stop her,
Father of ten slays nine with chopper,
Somebody's running to fetch the copper,
Bill Posters will be prosecuted.

Found in taxi with neighbour's wife,
You never had such a time in your life,
Bill Posters, O Bill Posters.
Helen who wrecked the Grecian ships
Was round as an apple about the hips
But a weasel bit from between her lips,
Bill Posters will be prosecuted.

Who was the hiker who dropped the match
And didn't believe the grass would catch,
Bill Posters, O Bill Posters?
The creeks are dry and there's nowhere to run,
A red smoke covers the face of the sun
And there in the murk of it justice is done,
Bill Posters will be prosecuted.

Wasn't it you, was it somebody else,
Adam and Eve as the fable tells,
Bill Posters, O Bill Posters?
Whoever it was it's you they'll blame,
It's you they'll throw to the house of flame,
Listen, the very stones proclaim
Bill Posters will be prosecuted.

Rage at the stars but they won't hear,
Venus shines for her dainty dear,
Bill Posters, O Bill Posters.
Saturn goes round in a ring all night,
Orion buckles his belt up tight,
There's a demon doctor at Mars' red light,
Bill Posters will be prosecuted.

38

Call to your brother, he's deaf as a post,
Call to your sister, she's gone like a ghost,
Bill Posters, O Bill Posters.
A man can't walk if a man can't fall,
Or maybe you did no harm at all,
But the writing is glaring on every wall,
Bill Posters will be prosecuted.

You shall be washed as white as snow
In a hundred million years or so
Bill Posters, O Bill Posters.
As white as a gull you shall rise from the slime,
But now you are living and life is crime,
You were born a man and you'll serve your time,
Bill Posters will be prosecuted.

THE NET

My wings were blue in the ocean green,
The prettiest things that ever were seen,
The gurnet said to the catfish.
Rose were my legs and rose my side
And who would have thought as I roved the tide
While the red crabs watched me scuttle or glide
I would come to dance in a net?

The fisherman sits by the water and chuckles,
Clams are his ears and limpets his knuckles,
The gurnet said to the catfish.
The beard of a mussel droops on his chin,
The scales of mackerel cling to his skin
And his eyes roll out and his eyes roll in
As he watches us dance in the net.

His eyes are hard as berries of kelp
But sweet is his daughter who comes to help,
The gurnet said to the catfish.
They take the ropes in their lean brown hands,
They haul us up on the shine of the sands
And the girl she laughs as the fisherman stands
And watches us dance in the net.

Let her hang up her clothes on a gooseberry-bush
For the waves say crash and the foam says hush,
The gurnet said to the catfish.
The surf is red with struggle and slaughter
And somewhere on earth or in sky or water
That scaly man and his long-legged daughter
Will dance like fish in a net.

There's a horrible man with a silver eye
Who stares like a demon out of the sky,
The gurnet said to the catfish.
The waves run here and the waves run there
But they can't escape that eye in the air,
And all of the seas in that silver flare
Must dance like fish in a net.

The fishes dance to the fisherman's tune,
The waters run to the pull of the moon,
The gurnet said to the catfish.
And there on the sand at the edge of the tide
The fisherman's daughter dancing in pride
With her rosy legs and her rosy side
Is less than a fish in a net.

Let her hide away in the deepest caves
Where the octopus threshes his arms and raves,
The gurnet said to the catfish.
Let her crouch with the drowned in the midnight pall
Where the starfish turns his face to the wall,
But water and woman and moon and all
They dance like fish in a net.

For somewhere glaring in wastes of space
There's a monstrous eye in an empty face,
The gurnet said to the catfish.
And round and round in the spell of that stare,
Splashing and flashing and biting the snare,
Go all the glittering shoals of the air
Dancing like fish in a net.

Somebody sits in space and chuckles
With hair like a comet's and stars for knuckles,
The gurnet said to the catfish.
Glimmer of side and swirl of fin,
His arms are huge as he hauls them in
And his teeth are a shark's in a mile-wide grin
As he watches them dance in the net.

There I am going and there go you,
I with my wings of butterfly-blue,
The gurnet said to the catfish.
The moon comes in and he swallows it whole,
Now it's the girl with the wings on her soul,
Now it's the fisher and the great eyes roll
As he watches him dance in the net.

HEAVEN IS A BUSY PLACE

Heaven is a busy place.
Those in a state of grace
Continually twanging the harp
And Court at eight-thirty sharp.
Did he do ill or well,
Shall he be sent to hell
That scoundrel in the dock?
The great black Judgment Book
Says nothing good of him;
Weeping of seraphim.

41

Twanging the harp and mourning.
Three more, a score for burning,
And always, if not the best,
Those of most interest.
And then the deputations—
Bishops for their congregations,
Relations and friends of cherubs,
Mahomet and all those Arabs . . .
Arrival with knocking knees
Of sixty thousand Chinese.

Incessant tinkle of strings.
And rain for Alice Springs
Now seven years in arrears.
Such multifarious cares,
Sparrows to be watched as they fall,
Elephants, ants and all
To the egg of the frog in the slime.
Then wind up the clock of time,
Douse the red sun in the deep,
Put the cat on the moon, and sleep.

Sir, I would make my petition:
Love and fulfilled ambition;
Some friends to be partly protected,
Some enemies grossly afflicted,
And, if I rise no higher,
A place at least by the fire.
But earth is a busy planet
And, failing the timely minute,
I found it best to postpone,
Do as well as I could on my own.

Now I have found a place
Where in their twisted grace
Soft-footed mangroves glide,
Fishing the green of the tide
With net and club and spear:
And all is so silent here
Lying by the gum-tree's root
I listen to a beetle's foot
Loud as a midnight thief
Crash on a fallen leaf.

If in the heavenly clime
They share such gaps in time,
Here if ever is the place
And the chance to state one's case.
But I must return a favour:
Life has a lovely flavour
And now there is time to waste
Now there is time to taste
(I think I shall not intrude)
Heaven is finding it good.

ROCK CARVING

The lines grow slack in our hands at full high-water;
The midnight rears in the sky; and beneath the boat
Another midnight, dwarfing the flare of a match
Or flare of a mind, expands and deepens. We float
Abandoned as driftwood on a tide that drowns all speech,
Where movement of hand or keel can make no mark
That will stand in space or endure one moment in time.
Flashing in shallows or hiding in murderous dark,

The fish live out their lives in weeds and silence;
And, locked like them in some alien struggle or peace,
No business of ours, from the moon to the water's edge,
Looming above us, tower the gigantic trees.
Among those rocks where time has ravaged the ridge,
In all that pattern cold and inhuman as the tide's,
Where shall the mind make camp? How in that darkness
Shall the mind ride tranquil with light as the high moon rides?

Shine the torch on the rock: we are not the first
Alone and lost in this world of water and stone.
See, though the maker's life has vanished like a leaf's,
The carvings living a hard strange life of their own
Above the water, beneath the tormented cliffs.
They glow with immortal being, as though the stone fish
May flap and slither to the tide, and the kangaroo
Bound from the rock and crash away through the bush.

The moon lights a thousand candles upon the water,
But none for the carver of stone; and nobody comes
Of his own long-scattered tribe to remember him
With dance and song and firelight under the gums;
But he walks again for me at the water's rim
And works at his rock, and a light begins to glow
Clear for his sake among the dark of my mind
Where the branches reach and the silent waters flow.

I watch him working through a summer afternoon,
Patient as the stone itself while his tribesmen sleep;
The children jostle, the girls cry out in the sun,
And first the fish and then the great 'roo take shape.
The work is crude, and he knows it; but now it is done;
And whoever laughs is a little afraid in the end,
For here is a swimmer in stone, and a beast that leaps
Nowhere for ever, and both can be touched with the hand.

I could have sat down with that man and talked about fishing,
How the bream are fish of the night, and they take the bait
With a run before you are ready; of the fabulous catches
For which we always got there a week too late;
And of how a man in the lonely midnight watches
Becomes himself a part of night and the tide
And, lost in the blackness, has need of a wife or a dog
Or a blackfellow's ghost to sit in peace by his side.

Centuries dead perhaps. But night and the water,
And the work of your hands on the rock have brought us together,
Fishermen both, and carvers both, old man.
I know as you how the work goes naked to the weather,
How we cut our thought into stone as best we can,
Laugh at our pain, and leave it to take its chance.
Maybe it's all for nothing, for the sky to look at,
Or maybe for us the distant candles dance.

The boat tugs at the kellick as it feels the ebb.
Good-bye, old wraith, and good luck. You did what you could
To leave your mark on stone like a mark on time,
That the sky in the mind and the midnight sea in the blood
Should be less of a desolation for the men to come;
And who can do more than you? Gone, you are gone;
But, dark a moment in the moonlight, your hand hovers,
And moves like the shadow of a bird across the stone.

THE DOSSER IN SPRINGTIME

That girl from the sun is bathing in the creek,
Says the white old dosser in the cave.
It's a sight worth seeing though your old frame's weak;
Her clothes are on the wattle and it's gold all over,
And if I was twenty I'd try to be her lover,
Says the white old dosser in the cave.

If I was twenty I'd chase her back to Bourke,
Says the white old dosser in the cave.
My swag on my shoulder and a haughty eye for work,
I'd chase her to the sunset where the desert burns and reels,
With an old blue dog full of fleas at my heels,
Says the white old dosser in the cave.

I'd chase her back to Bourke again, I'd chase her back to Alice,
Says the white old dosser in the cave.
And I'd drop upon her sleeping like a beauty in a palace
With the sunset wrapped around her and a black snake keeping
    watch—
She's lovely and she's naked but she's very hard to catch,
Says the white old dosser in the cave.

I've been cooling here for years with the gum-trees wet and weird,
Says the white old dosser in the cave.
My head grew lichens and moss was my beard,
The creek was in my brain and a bullfrog in my belly,
The she-oaks washed their hair in me all down the gloomy gully,
Says the white old dosser in the cave.

My eyes were full of water and my ears were stopped with bubbles,
Says the white old dosser in the cave.
Yabbies raised their claws in me or skulked behind the pebbles.
The water-beetle loved his wife, he chased her round and round—
I thought I'd never see a girl unless I found one drowned,
Says the white old dosser in the cave.

Many a time I laughed aloud to stop my heart from thumping,
Says the white old dosser in the cave.
I saw my laugh I saw my laugh I saw my laugh go jumping
Like a jaunty old goanna with his tail up stiff
Till he dived like a stone in the pool below the cliff,
Says the white old dosser in the cave.

46

There's a fine bed of bracken, the billy boils beside her,
Says the white old dosser in the cave.
But no one ever ate with me except the loathsome spider;
And no one ever lay with me beside the sandstone wall
Except the pallid moonlight and she's no good at all,
Says the white old dosser in the cave.

But now she's in the creek again, that woman made of flame,
Says the white old dosser in the cave.
By cripes, if I was twenty I'd stop her little game.
Her dress is on the wattle—I'd take it off and hide it;
And when she sought that golden dress, I'd lay her down beside it,
Says the white old dosser in the cave.

THE BISHOP

Robed and mitred the bishop stands and hard by his ear a pigeon
Preens in the sun on top of his head and tells him about religion.

Oh, Time has struck the bishop stiff with its eye as cold as a
    Gorgon's,
His ·body is bronze and his heart is too (if a statue contains such
    organs);

Yet who can tell if the bishop's soul like a white frost-bitten petal
Fell dead that day or flurried away or now in this shell of metal

Glimmers behind those benignant eyes, in the hollow breast still
    lingers
And wavers and burns like rays of the sun from the outstretched
    hand and fingers.

On some improbable raft no doubt the bishop through life went
    skimming
(The waters are dark and the waves are high and we all grow tired
    of swimming);

47

But now he stands on a rock indeed, his coat will turn all weather,
He and the earth and the stars themselves will stand or fall together.

A man alive is a narrow man however he tries to hide it,
He sets up a wall to keep him safe and the heathen rage outside it;

And a saint alive is a narrow saint, soaring alone like a steeple,
But here is a man as broad as the sun, shining on all the people.

No one has heard his mouth of bronze open for groan or curse
As an ambulance rushed a child to be born or a corpse went by in
    a hearse;

No one has heard him stamp on his plinth with a harsh metallic
    foot
As Sarah staggers to William Street before the wine-bars shut;

No one has heard him shudder and clank when free at last from
    the ship
Bill goes rolling to Palmer Street with a bottle parked on his hip.

Alike to him are the roaring bus with wharfies up from the 'Loo
And the plump old girl the chauffeur drives to the home with the
    Harbour view;

Smith of the suburbs reading his paper, escaping by tram from the
    boss,
The trim little bits with their scarlet nails homing to flats at the
    Cross;

The rich and the poor, the strong and the weak, the priest and
    sinner and sot,
Whether they like it or whether they don't the bishop blesses the
    lot.

The crowds on Sundays may pass him by with never a glance or
nod
(The orators rave in the Dom. today and one of them might be
God),

But high on his perch the bishop stands, serving whoever needs:
He and the saintly peanut man are above the battle of creeds.

I mightn't have liked the bishop alive but I certainly like him
dead,
The good old man in his suit of bronze with the pigeon on top of
his head;

Solid in space, secure in time, defiant he takes his stand,
The whole of life goes blessed on its way beneath the sun of his
hand.

EXTRACTS FROM
FIVE VERSE PLAYS

From THE FIRE ON THE SNOW
THE END OF THE JOURNEY

SCOTT. I am glad we have lived so bitterly and die so hard;
    And if only they find what I've written, perhaps our story
    Will say what I wanted to say; that a man must learn
    To endure agony, to endure and endure again
    Until agony itself is beaten out into joy.

    Facing this certain death these last two days,
    Writing these farewell letters to friends and the world,
    I have seen our lives as a drowning man would see them,
    I have seen them whole, and there's nothing I would change.
    Do you remember it all, remember living?

WILSON. I remember the ship going out, so much more daring
    Than the gulls that so quickly scudded back to the port.

SCOTT. I remember before that, vaguely, England. It seems
    A blue mist, and hollows where leaves were green
    And everyone was kind, you could touch their hands.
    That was years ago. I remember more clearly
    New Zealand, that garden at Christchurch, how sharply blue
    The peaks of the Kaikouras stabbed the horizon,
    And the Avon looked so tranquil among its willows,
    And the city was quiet. But that was years ago.
    I remember the ship, yes; shouting and the gulls,
    And in such a little while no gulls or shouting,
    But the sea darkening and looking lonely. Wilson,
    Remember those days in the pack, the sun on the ice
    And the men's voices clear as bells as they sang,
    Clear as bells.

WILSON. The ice was dazzling white and the sea was blue,
    A very dark blue, and all the sailors were singing.
    I remember the winter, the comradeship in the hut,
    But it faded out. We were cold. Those long dark days
    When nobody spoke and we felt like dreams and shadows.

SCOTT. One night I walked to the cliffs alone, and the moon
    Was pure and burning on those frozen spires and crags,
    So that they leapt like flames. The ice was blazing.
    And the hut, when I came back, was a red island,
    A ship at sea, a fire of human beings,
    Warm and secure. But that was years ago.
    I remember the march to the Pole beginning; sledges,
    Dogs, ponies, the happy cavalcade,
    The long swinging easy marches, the feeling
    Of songs and banners.
    I remember the black flag that told us about Amundsen,
    That fatal day.

WILSON.   We shouldn't have cared.

SCOTT.   But we did,
    And the Pole was ghosts and ruins, and the snow on our mouths
    Was ashes, ashes. And Evans crumbled away,
    And the Soldier after him.
                        How am I justified,
    Wilson, how am I justified for Oates and Evans,
    And Bowers . . . and you?

WILSON.   All of us chose to do it,
    Our own will brought us, our death on the ice
    Was foreseen by each of us; accepted. Let your mind be at peace.
    I have seen this death as the common fate made clearer,
    And cleaner, too, this simple struggle on the ice.
    We dreamed, we so nearly triumphed, we were defeated
    As every man in some great or humble way
    Dreams, and nearly triumphs, and is always defeated,
    And then, as we did, triumphs again in endurance.
    Triumph is nothing; defeat is nothing; life is
    Endurance; and afterwards, death. And whatever death is,
    The endurance remains like a fire, a sculpture, a mountain
    To hearten our children. I tell you,
    Such a struggle as ours is living; it lives after death
    Purely, like flame, a thing burning and perfect.

SCOTT. There was something else. I can't remember now;
I am tired. Death is very near me.

                             Wilson,
There is something else, something to do with me.
Moonlight on ice. Wilson—

                      Wilson!

                          Agony.
Two dead men; and a dying man remembering
The burning snow, the crags towering like flame.

From NED KELLY
IN SHERRITT'S HUT

THE SERGEANT. Mrs Sherritt, and you, too, Mrs Barry, I warn you:
Go easy on Aaron tonight. Be soft with the lad;
Whatever he's done, and however he'll have to pay for it,
He's walking in the terror of death, and that's a place
That's high and lonely as the moon, if the moon could fall.
Bring him to earth, but gently.

RITA.   What's wrong with you, sergeant?
We know he's got the wind up.

THE SERGEANT.   It's more than that.
When the super told him that demon of a woman Byrne
Had been bending over, staring and glaring at his face,
And him asleep all the while,
The lad turned white, the cold sweat broke out
Like rain on his forehead, he struggled to speak and couldn't.
'Twas the tongue of a dead man he was trying to speak with,
And Aaron knew it.

55

RITA.   You never told us this.

THE SERGEANT. "Now I'm a dead man." That's what he said,
When his tongue came back to life. "I'm a dead man."
Go easy on him.
   [AARON SHERRITT *appears in the open doorway. He is young,
   light-haired, stockily built and wears a dirty white shirt and
   corduroy trousers tucked into his boots. He looks careworn
   and desperate; or, in moments of optimism, shifty.
   As he enters,* RITA *moves towards him in an impulse of tender-
   ness, then pauses, preferring to release her fears in nagging.*]

RITA (*sharply*). Aaron! Why didn't you answer?

SHERRITT.   Why were you screaming?
  What the hell did you shout for, sergeant?

RITA.   I told him to.

SHERRITT. You fool, you can hear for miles on a night like this.
Stand at the door and bellow—
They mightn't have heard you before. They might be deaf.
Tell them I'm here. Go and shout it down the gully.

RITA. They know where we live.

SHERRITT.   They'll know I'm at home, too,
  When you howl my name through the bush.

RITA.   Don't pick on me.

MRS BARRY. Go out and pick on the moon. It's your own madness,
  Not Rita, that's done the harm.

RITA.   Be quiet, mother.

THE SERGEANT. You heard nothing, Sherritt?

56

SHERRITT.   What could I hear
    When you kicked up such a shindy! I thought I heard
    Something, it might have been horses, I heard a splashing
    Like horses crossing the creek. I couldn't tell.
    The bush is so stiff with the frost it cracks like glass;
    The bark cracking and the sticks snapping and your boots
    As loud as cattle on the leaves. When you stop and listen,
    The noises stop. I thought I heard them coming,
    But they stopped when I stopped to listen, or else it was nothing.
    I don't know what it was.
        [*He sits at the table, despairing.* RITA *goes to him and strokes
        his head.*]

RITA. Poor old Aaron.

SHERRITT (*clasping her hand*). Rita!

RITA.   You're as cold as ice.

SHERRITT (*letting her hand fall and jumping to his feet*). I'm cold to
    the bone. But it's better out in the open
    Than trapped in here.

THE SERGEANT.   You're as safe as a bank, man.

MRS BARRY. That's just what Aaron's afraid of.

THE SERGEANT.   What more do you want?
    There's four police in the house.

RITA.   Three asleep,
    And one with the wind up.

SHERRITT.   I want the Kellys dead.

MRS BARRY. That's a happy thought to sleep with.

SHERRITT.   I want them dead.
    We won't sleep till they are.

THE SERGEANT.   You'll see them dead,
   Your cobber dancing in the sky along with the others.

RITA. Don't rub it in.

MRS BARRY.   The Kellys were born to be hanged.
   And so was Joe Byrne.

SHERRITT.   I could lie behind a rock
   And they'd pass me and never notice. I'll camp in the bush.

RITA. You're not going out again; I won't let you.

SHERRITT. The shack's a death-trap. They can sneak right up to the
      door.
   I won't have a chance. I could keep a watch in the bush.

RITA. While we stay here and chance it? Not on your life.
   We'll stick together.

SHERRITT.   You can come with me, Rita.
   No, you'd better stay here. Too many would spoil it,
   You'd kick up too much row. Stay in the shack.
   You'll be all right.

MRS BARRY.   Stay here and have our throats cut?
   Not that I mind—it'll be a change to be murdered.

SHERRITT. You're safe enough, Mrs Barry.

RITA.   If the Kellys come
   And you're not here, they're sure to turn on us.
   We'll all be killed.

THE SERGEANT.   They'd never hurt a woman.
   You can take my word for that. I know the Kellys,
   They're not so bad in their way. It's your husband they want,
   The lad that sold them.

58

RITA.   And hasn't been paid, either.

SHERRITT. We'll camp in the bush. What do you say, sergeant?
    You and I will find a hide-out down the gully.
    The blokes in the bedroom there can guard the women.

THE SERGEANT. If you're sleeping with Mrs Green, go by yourself;
    She's a frosty bitch tonight. I'm off to my bunk.

SHERRITT. It isn't safe to be sleeping. We'll have to watch.

THE SERGEANT. If you make as good a sentry as you have informer,
    We can all sleep sound enough. I leave it to you.

RITA. You have no right to do it.

THE SERGEANT.   You see that door?
    That's where I'll be, Mrs Sherritt. It's not so far
    You couldn't reach it to knock, it's not so thick
    We'll not be able to hear you. If the Kellys come
    For the lad that betrayed them, we'll be there to save his wife.

SHERRITT. You've got to get me away.

THE SERGEANT.   And don't we intend to?
    You wouldn't want to be running away in the night
    Like a man that's done a murder.

SHERRITT.   I've got to get out.

THE SERGEANT. Now that you've joined us, lad, you trust the police.
    Sure, we know it, there's not much room in Australia
    For a man that's squealed on his mates. We'll see you escape,
    We'll pack you off to America, safe with your money.
    You'll be living like a lord on the fortune you got for the Kellys
    And the ghosts won't cross the water. But you see, Aaron,
    The Kellys aren't captured yet, so you'll have to wait.

RITA. You're trying to beat him. You won't part out with the money.

MRS BARRY. The sergeant hasn't got it.

THE SERGEANT.   We'll pay the reward
    As soon as it's due.

SHERRITT.   You've got to get me away.
    You can send the money after.

THE SERGEANT.   We might do that,
    There's time enough. You can't bustle the law.

RITA. You're against him now. You weren't against him before
    When you wheedled and crawled to get your information,
    Smiling and slapping his back, shouting him drinks,
    Blackmailing, promising, edging him into a corner
    Till you had him where you wanted and slipped on the bridle.
    You ride him hard now.

SHERRITT.   They're all against me.
    The Kellys, the traps, the people wherever I go.
    The last few weeks I've drunk by myself. They're scared
    To talk to me in the pubs, or else they're against me.
    Pretty soon the dogs will lift up their heads and howl
    When they see me coming. I'm done, and I smell of death.

From THE GOLDEN LOVER
TAWHAI AND WHANA

WHANA. On the cold sands of my life, between the forest
    Where all is sombre, and the water where all is death,
    You, the white heron, sacred and solitary,
    And all that the world holds of grace and beauty
    Shining where the light strikes on your folded wings.
    Ah, keep them folded, Tawhai. Do not fly away.

TAWHAI. I do not think I would go now if I could.
　　What do they call you?

WHANA.　　　　　　　　　Whana. My name is Whana.

TAWHAI. Whana. The wild name, the wild name,
　　Like a stone in a mountain stream.

WHANA.　　　　　　　　　　Ah, you are perfect!

TAWHAI. No, do not touch me yet. How do I know
　　That all your beautiful words are not a snare
　　Of the faery people? Is it truly me you love,
　　Or were you not waiting there on the edge of the forest
　　For any woman of my people not as ugly as Koura?

WHANA. Eh, that old kiwi, how she scuttled for her life in the
　　　　morning!
　　But I waited for you, Tawhai, you with the wings.
　　How many weeks have I watched you at work in the fields,
　　Ventured at night to the pa reeking of your people,
　　Yearning to see you, burning for a chance like this.

TAWHAI. You watched and waited for me! But why for me?
　　There are many beautiful women among the Maoris,
　　Or nearly beautiful.

WHANA.　　　　　But only one white heron.
　　Tawhai, I love you.

TAWHAI.　　　　　But why?

WHANA.　　　　　　　　When the tui sings,
　　The bell through the green of the forest, clear and deep,
　　Some form arises trembling among the music
　　Like a silver ghost, my darling. You are that ghost.
　　When the kowhai breaks into flower and the honied blossoms
　　Flow down to the earth in a waterfall still and silent,

61

Some form that is not a tree laughs there and sings
And bathes her hair and her hands in the golden pool:
Your hair and your hands, you heart of the spring and its flowers.
A green spirit in the forest, a dark in the earth,
A fire of silver burning now with the stars—
Tawhai, Tawhai, you are all the earth and the heavens.

TAWHAI. To me in my life no one has said such things.
It is sweet to be here with you in the bush and moonlight
And to hear you speak. Eh, my wild Whana
With your strange name and your mountain torrent of words
And your auburn hair, fierce face and body of gold,
You might indeed be a lover out of a dream.

WHANA. You are not a woman beside me but the earth burning.
Your dark hair smoulders, and your body under my hand
Is all one flame. And yet how the blaze takes form!
It is not the long loose wandering flame of aurora
Rose and green when the sky catches fire in winter,
That stretches far out of reach and shrinks as you watch it;
That is the flame of your spirit. But the fire of your body,
It is here, it is close, I can touch it, ember and flame.
See how it branches, the lovely leap and the flash
In your arm, your hand, the wavering light of your fingers,
And there, where your mouth is, the glowing heart of the
    embers;
And the long, adorable, curving streamers of flame
Flowing to your breast and down the lines of your body,
Then branching again. Fire of the sky in your spirit,
Fire of the earth in your body! Tawhai, Tawhai,
Our spirits met in the burning sky together
How long ago! And now you are mine on earth.
And I, I am fire like yourself; these hands of mine
Can hold you and not be afraid, not wither to ash.
See, I can lift you, fire in a cradle of fire,
And take you away to be my own for ever.

From SHIPWRECK
CORNELIUS FOR SENTENCE

PELSART. You are the prisoner Cornelius.
The last. Well, I have seen it out. Prisoner,
You must not expect to escape due retribution.

CORNELIUS. At Batavia, yes; put my case to the Company, eh,
When you send me there with the others. Like old times,
When I sail with you in the morning. Must travel in irons;
Not quite what it was; used to be free on deck,
Out in the sun, watching the blue water
And the albatross that hung in the air by the rail
So close you could almost touch him, as big as a goose.

PELSART. You should not hope to sail on the sea again.

CORNELIUS. But I must. It's my life. Cornelius, the supercargo.
You know me. You used to speak. Remember, you watched me,
Useful, bustling the men, make jokes and laugh.
You remember, Commodore?

PELSART. Yes, I remember, prisoner;
And also what has happened since. I have your confession.

CORNELIUS. You wrenched it out on the rack.

PELSART. Do you withdraw it?

APELDOORN. I should be glad to examine the prisoner further
—If he requires it—by means of the same instrument.

CORNELIUS. Instrument, yes, that's good. You stretched me out
Like the gut of a fiddle. I played you the tune you asked for.

PELSART. Do you withdraw then?

CORNELIUS. No. Had enough of that.

63

PELSART. I shall proceed to sentence.

CORNELIUS.   No. It's me.
   Don't say it. You'd hang me. You couldn't do it, Commodore.
   Me; here; I'm alive. Fat belly I've got;
   Can talk; laugh like an owl . . . and this afternoon,
   One hour away, like Seevanck, just to go out.
   All this, my body, body of a toad I know,
   But I fed it, even washed it sometimes, covered it in silk,
   Gave it water and wine—more wine than water when I could—
   Good old belly and body, you couldn't kill it.
   To die, that's not too good; that's to be nothing:
   Like a hawk or a weasel you see on a farmer's fence,
   Dried, like a rag; somebody's played them a joke,
   So they'll steal no more of the chickens: the joke of death.

APELDOORN. Death is at your elbow, prisoner.

CORNELIUS (*startled; quickly glancing behind him*). Ha, you say so!
   That's a black shadow for a man; no friend of mine.
   I kept better company once. Bad, I know;
   Huyssen when he laughed you heard the bark of the fox;
   But still, I liked them; good fellows, like all the bad ones.
   I was bad myself; not big and dangerous though;
   Would have made a good poacher: not rob your house,
   Not lurk on a dark road, but roam in your park
   With a snare for the soft little hare; come home, perhaps,
   With a pheasant stuffed in my shirt: the little fellows,
   Nice taste, and not much harm. I liked to drink;
   Who doesn't? And a change from the wife sometimes. My fun.
   And money, and not too honestly. Bit here, bit there,
   Put out your hand and take it and soon there's a pile:
   Nothing for a great merchant, but something for me,
   I don't want much: you can read the great book just as well
   With the stub of a candle. Besides, I'm a lazy fellow:
   I talked in the sun and life sat down for company.
   Wasn't it so on the ship? Made other men work,
   But I was a great loafer. Oh, I was bad!

64

PELSART (*in a thin shout of rage*). You unspeakable murderous
    villain!

CORNELIUS.   Couldn't be; couldn't!

PELSART. That morning of massacre, a hundred men and women,
    The shriek of terror in the air and the groans of the dying,
    The frenzy and the carnage; on the clean grass and the sand
    The wounded threshing in their blood and the dead contorted.
    Van Mylen and all the others; a hundred massacred
    By you in your bestial fury. And then Claes Harman,
    And the horrible rape of his wife. And then Sebastian.
    And night after night, here in my tent, plotting
    To massacre Hays, you bloody beast out of hell.

CORNELIUS (*frenzied*). Stop! You're a liar! Look at my hand. Look!
    Killed not one of them; white. (*Raising both hands and shaking
    the right at his accusers*) My hand! My hand!

APELDOORN. Look at it while you can.

CORNELIUS.   Yes, you'll chop it!
    Bait me. You bait the bull. Like dogs around me.
    This tent. I was master here; and all the island.
    They know what I am; a king. A king among them.

APELDOORN. King Cornelius, I think your reign is over.

CORNELIUS. You twist your fingers in my brains; you tear out my
    heart.
    I'm alone. You all accuse me. You howl for my death.
    And I did not do it. I couldn't have done such things.
    You won't see it. Look at what I am—a man.
    Like anyone else. Good fellow. Some devil did it!

PELSART. Then go to the home of devils!

    [LUCRETIA *stands up as if to leave the tent.*]

65

JUDITH (*catching her hand*).   Wait, Lucretia.

LUCRETIA (*with hushed anger*). No, let me go.

CORNELIUS.   Lucretia——

APELDOORN.   Prisoner, silence!

PELSART. There is no need to stay, Madam van Mylen.
   This is distressing to you.

LUCRETIA.   I suppose it is.
   Oh, I don't know. I don't feel anything much.
   I want to be out in the air.

CORNELIUS (*as she begins to go*). I couldn't tell you;
   Gave me no chance. I loved you.

LUCRETIA (*in a low voice*).   This fellow is dead.

CORNELIUS. No, don't say it; don't go. If I'd been young
   And handsome like Huyssen I might have known how to say it
   And you to believe it. I loved you most when you hated me;
   So proud, so white, so deadly, so far from my reach.
   Loved you in fear, when you trembled; I bled for you then,   •
   Could have struck myself with a knife. So simply loved you,
   Tenderly, smiling, when I saw you playing with your cat.
   And how to say it with the wildcat blazing in your eyes?
   I wouldn't have touched you; waited; some day you'd have seen;
   Or let you go in the end; but these things happen:
   Wrong from the start, so go on making them worse
   Till all's a ruin and you hate me. You'll never know
   The honour I paid you in my heart: so steadfast you were,
   So sweetly in love with van Mylen. Ah, well, hate me!
   I'm the devil. Sebastian said it. The fiend in my heart.

LUCRETIA. No. I don't hate you, Cornelius. You can die in peace;
   But die, but die, die! They'll leave you on the gallows
   Like a tongue in the bell of the sky, the voice of this rock

66

Crying and clanging in a silent music of anguish
And if I were still on this island it might be a sweet
Or a harsh or a pitiful sound, but we sail at daybreak
And I'll never hear it. Not a whisper. I hope to forget you.

[*She goes out.*]

CORNELIUS (*awed*). Ah, then it's death.

PELSART (*more gently*).   Yes, prisoner, it is.

CORNELIUS. The strange thing. Black. Not to be king any more.

PELSART. These are strange crimes, Cornelius, that you have
    committed;
    Unreasonable, mad. I do not quite understand them.
    As if you thought somehow to escape the reckoning,
    As if this speck of rock in the middle of the sea
    Were all the world, some cage of God's in space
    Where beast met beast in frenzy and nobody cared
    Who roared in triumph or what in defeat lay mangled.

CORNELIUS. Me to be mangled now. Not even to be man.
    Not me. But what? What to be now? That thing
    On the gallows. Black. Swinging. Without its hand.
    Flying, like a black seagull; nowhere. Always.
    Day after day. In the sun at the edge of the water.
    But a cave, a darkness; not feeling the warmth of the sun,
    Not watching the waves. The seagulls will have my eyes.
    And David beside me, Seevanck; hanging together
    Like shadows on the tall gallows, not saying a word:
    As if he was no one; and I beside him nobody.
    Commodore, don't. Don't do it!

PELSART.   My duty, prisoner.

CORNELIUS. We were mad; the blood and the shouting; after you left
    The whole island was mad.

PELSART. I think that is true.

My own men, seamen! But, madness or not,
I have returned to restore sanity and discipline
And you must die. It has been an unlucky voyage.
I cannot pity you, prisoner; but sometimes, my friends,
I am sorry for the race of man, trapped on this planet.
A man alive must act, must think and do,
And stand to a harsh judgment for what he does.
Decision, action, judgment.

From FISHER'S GHOST
FISHER TO WORRALL

Where are you, George, where are you, George,
Oh can't you hear me singing?
Come out of the night wherever you are,
I want to see you swinging.

You were a kind of mate of mine,
You'd never do me harm,
And you followed me from the Black Sheep Inn
And murdered me for my farm.

You followed me in the dead of night
And waited under the gumtree
And knocked me down with a batten, George,
A shame to all the country.

You sold my cows and my horses too,
The good bay mare and the sorrel
And you stole the cash in the biscuit-tin,
And you shall pay, George Worrall.

Oh there are crowds in Sydney Town
The hard old lags and the soldiers
And you shall hang on the gallows tree,
A joy to all beholders.

The bearded sailors, the immigrant boys,
The drabs and the starving Irish,
They'll fill themselves with grog this day
And cheer as they watch you perish.

Listen, I hear the beating drum,
Listen, I hear the bell
And splashing across the cool Tank Stream
The crowd climb up the hill.

They climb the hill to the Blue Post Inn
They line The Rocks for the view,
And they'll drink and yell as they see you swing,
And good enough for you too.

Oh let me see you riding now
The gallows tree so high:
George Worrall, you killed Fisher's ghost;
George Worrall, you must die.

THE BLACKTRACKER'S STORY

There is a thing that I have found
In the creek of Fisher's ghost
Would make a white man blench with fear
And a black man run, almost.

It is a creek like other creeks
(Fisher's ghost is lonely)
That sleeps on sandy beds for weeks
Or stumbles where it's stony.

Through paddocks brown, through crops of corn
(Oh where is Fisher now?)
I followed it and thought it knew
A thing no creek should know.

I saw the little clear brown pool
(Oh where is Fisher buried?)
Where water-beetles chase the sun
And dragonflies are married.

I saw the floating water-spinners
(What's that beneath the rocks?)
Whose shadows lie on the sand below
Like footfalls of a fox.

I saw the mudhole in the bank
(It seemed a thing to fear)
And there the yabbie crawled to drink
With claws out like a spear.

The moon was on the standing corn
(Fisher's ghost is lonely)
And every pool and easy turn
The creek was white and moony.

I took a sheaf I stripped the leaf
(Dead man's fat floats up)
And skimmed that cold white water there
And drank it like a cup.

Lord come and wash you, little creek,
From mountain to the coast,
For I have tasted murder there
In the creek of Fisher's ghost.

From

GLENCOE

1947

"The word that's come frae the English king
Is sudden and sharp and hard:
'Ye must take my oath by the day I set
Or suffer by fire and sword'."

"Then easy now, my youngest son,
Ye needna be sae squeamish;
Maybe they'll burn a barn or twa,
Maybe a wee bit skirmish."

"I see Breadalbane's hand in this,
The evil web o' the spider;
He covets MacIan's gear and beasts,
Your mountainside and your river."

"Then easy now, my lady wife,
The Coe runs strong in its foam
And I've a target o' tough bull's hide
Shall cover my house and home."

"I'd swear no oath for the Dutchman king
Who sits on a Scotsman's throne;
But out like the wild MacGregor men
I'd fight in the hills by my lone."

"Then easy now, my good son John,
The Stewart's owre the water;
And I'll take the oath if he gives me leave
And I'll do my fighting later."

"But late's the day and late's the hour
And Jamie sends nae word;
The rowan reddens owre the burn
And the frost sets white and hard."

"Then easy now, my son's fair wife,
There's time for a messenger yet;
Lochiel, Appin, Keppoch, Glengarry,
We'll all be in by the date."

"Well for the lads that hunt the deer
And follow the Coe for salmon;
But wae for the wife and the ragged bairns
That bide in the henchman's cabin."

"Then easy now, my clansmen all,
I hae no will for the thing
But I'll take the oath when the word comes through
Frae Scotland's rightful king."

"Oh, see ye no' delay too long,
See ye no' delay,
For dark's the shadow on hall and clan
If ye're no' come in by the day."

5

The Earl of Breadalbane seems to flinch
And his periwig rises half an inch;
The fingers spread and the features blanch
Of the black Earl of Breadalbane.

Still is the eye of the bird of prey
Yet it seems to widen, then close this day:
"He was two days late—is it truth ye say?"
Says the black Earl of Breadalbane.

Slowly the Earl of Breadalbane stands,
His fingers crook on his stretching hands:
"The Clan MacIan and all their lands!"
Says the black Earl of Breadalbane.

"There's an ancient war of clan and clan,
They thieved my cattle and dirked my kin,
And then there's a promise I made that man,"
Says the black Earl of Breadalbane.

"MacIan, that great red insolent bear
With the cunning of hell in his sleepy stare,
Who laughed in my face when I bade him beware
The power of the Earl of Breadalbane."

The Earl of Breadalbane paces the room,
Darkens his face with the cloud of doom:
"The king must agree but we'll manage him,"
Says the black Earl of Breadalbane.

"Ye can take my word to the Master of Stair,
Breadalbane comes with a secret to share
For the old red fox put his foot in the snare,"
Says the black Earl of Breadalbane.

"The old red fox in the mountain mist;
And two days late—he's lost, he's lost!"
And the Earl of Breadalbane closes his fist,
The black Earl of Breadalbane.

6

Round and gentle and dark and plump
Like a fat little bird in a blackberry clump,
Smiling face but eyes of care:
John Dalrymple, Master of Stair.

Bright with ribbon and ready to hand,
Stacked in holes of the desk and mind,
Papers here and documents there:
John Dalrymple, Master of Stair.

Secretary of the Scottish State,
King's adviser and lord of fate—
Scotland's turmoil and Europe's war:
John Dalrymple, Master of Stair.

Kill or be killed at this man's bidding—
What's the dream in those brown eyes hiding,
Framed in the periwig's powdered hair,
John Dalrymple, Master of Stair?

Strands run out from paper to paper,
The blackberry bush it spreads like a creeper;
Tangled in trouble and scratched with fear:
John Dalrymple, Master of Stair.

Peace in Scotland and rebels down
Or William loses the English crown,
And James comes back and where, oh, where,
Is John Dalrymple, Master of Stair?

When Highland rebels harry the border
Out goes decency, out goes order:
That the popish thief MacIan should dare—
Clan MacIan, beware, beware.

The dark eyes narrow, the soft lips twitch,
They say Dalrymple's dam is a witch;
The blackberry clump is the weasel's lair:
John Dalrymple, Master of Stair.

A lean dark woman she had two sons
And one of them died by poison once;
One's in his grave and the other is here:
John Dalrymple, Master of Stair.

Strands of blackberry twist and tangle;
Deep, oh, deep in the heart of the jungle,
Dark eyes flashing and tooth laid bare:
John Dalrymple, Master of Stair.

7

"So big MacIan has made a slip
And laid himself in the tiger's grip,"
Dalrymple said to Breadalbane.
"You'll guard the passes so none escape
And, man, it's your plan to maul them.

"The white cold snow is over the earth,
MacIan is snug with drink and mirth,"
Dalrymple said to Breadalbane.
"The cotter takes his cow to his hearth
And now is time to maul them.

"I stand for peace, I stand for law,
I've held MacIan from the tiger's claw,"
Dalrymple said to Breadalbane.
"But man, oh, man you tempt me now,
For, Lord, I would like to maul them.

"Do it, do it, fiend or man,
Burn the houses, ravage the clan,"
Dalrymple said to Breadalbane.
"I've waited for this since time began,
Waited my hour to maul them.

"You'll leave no chance that the birds take wing,
But make it a sweet and secretive thing,"
Dalrymple said to Breadalbane.
"I'll screw the word from the dull Dutch king
And, man, I think we'll maul them!"

8

Heavily droops the long Dutch nose,
Heavily hangs the wig:
"I cannot breathe in your London stews,
I cannot think in your fog."

Lined and pale is the long Dutch face,
Black is his coat and sober:
"I fight the French in the Protestant cause;
What is this Scottish robber?

"I do not know of your Highland feuds
Nor yet your clan MacDonald;
If it will cure with fire and swords
Why should our state be troubled?"

Heavily close the sad Dutch eyes,
Slowly nods the head:
"It seems like death for a few of these,
But I have seen many dead.

"A barbarous country, a barbarous race;
You say the man is a rebel:
What do I care what methods you use?"
The Dutchman thumps the table.

9

"Oho, oho,
We know, we know,"
The weasel said to the tiger.
"A king may sit on a velvet throne
But he turns his head when you twist his crown,
For you and I are men of affairs
And we know how things are done."

"When you need a man he is easy found,"
The tiger said to the weasel.
"I've a cousin that owes me twa-three pound;
And it shows you the way the kind gods smile,
He's a captain that serves my Lord Argyle.

"I'll send Glenlyon with Argyle's men,"
The tiger said to the weasel,
"To visit MacIan down in the glen;
And I wouldna wait to see that show
If I was a stone in the glen o' Glencoe."

"Oho, oho,
We know, we know!"
The weasel said to the tiger.
"I like the taste of your blood-red wine
And as for the fool in the lonely glen—
Well, you and I are men of the world
And we know how things are done."

10

Take Loch Linnhe's wavelets and put them in a sack,
Murmur on the shoreline and morning's silver smile,
Swinging from Fort William and past the Appin track
Gay with pipes and pennants come the soldiers of Argyle.

Sparkling stand the mountains, singing runs the Coe,
Snow is in the high notes and water in the low,
And skirling up the valley, row by kilted row,
A hundred bonny soldiers go marching to Glencoe.

Hey, Lieutenant Lindsay! Hey for Sergeant Barber!
He's the man to trim your beard with dagger or with sword;
Up the stony mountain the panting soldiers labour,
Green like floating branches gleams the tartan in the ford.

Someone took the pine-tree, someone took the heather,
With green and purple juices they dyed the hairy wool;
And jaunty in their bonnets with kilts that swing together
March the Campbells' soldiers by waterfall and pool.

Run, you black-faced ewes, now; stare you shaggy cattle;
Seldom breaks the silence here with kettledrums all drumming;
Is it avalanche or flood, is it distant sounds of battle,
The thunder in the mountains when the Campbell men are coming?

Whose the shade that stalks there beside King William's flag?
Glenlyon never threw it nor the feeble chief Argyle:
Take the screaming eagle and put him in a bag,
Breadalbane's power comes nearer up the darkening defile.

II

"Oh, come ye in war or come ye in peace,
Glenlyon, Robert Campbell?
For ye've come to where the knife-edge is,
Campbell that comes to MacDonald."
          "And why should I come to the edge of the knife
          When your ain son took my niece to wife?"

"Oh, who was it sent ye to wild Glencoe,
Glenlyon, Robert Campbell?
For never yet except as a foe
Campbell came to MacDonald."
          "Since ye gave your oath to the good Dutch king
          Ye may say he takes ye under his wing."

"When I gave my oath it was two days late,
Glenlyon, Robert Campbell.
Ye wouldna hae come on account o' that,
Campbell that comes to MacDonald?"
          "A poor old soldier he takes his orders;
          Ye'd no' begrudge us our winter quarters?"

"Oh, I hae bannocks and I hae beef,
Glenlyon, Robert Campbell,
But your kinsman called me rebel and thief,
Campbell that comes to MacDonald."
          "And should ye hae borrowed the Campbells' cows
          It's the better I'll eat in your auld stone house."

80

"Yet I hae meadows and I hae land,
Glenlyon, Robert Campbell;
And the Earl o' Breadalbane's a grasping hand,
Campbell that comes to MacDonald."
          "I eat no earth and I sip no frost,
          But I'll take a wee drap wi' a friendly host."

"Then I hae room and room to spare,
Glenlyon, Robert Campbell;
And aye there's a wee sma' keg to share,
So come ye in to MacDonald."

12

          "A card for you and a card for me,"
          And I'm no' the man that I used to be,
          And damn the Earl o' Breadalbane.
          Your two tall sons go prowling round
          But the devil's hoofprints canna be found
          Though he's here this night to maul them.

          "A glass to clink on your ain good glass,"
          And I'm no' the man that I once was,
          And pox on the Earl o' Breadalbane.
          Your lady she sits by the fire o' peat,
          Her face is old and fierce and sweet
          And her hair is grey and golden.

          "A win for you and a loss for me,"
          And I'm no' the man that I used to be,
          And a plague on the Earl o' Breadalbane.
          Two silken dresses against the dark,
          For there's my niece with her needlework,
          And I trust no ill befall them.

"Then where's the harm in another dram?"
And I dinna much like the man I am,
And damn the Earl o' Breadalbane.
I mind they painted my portrait once
In a velvet coat with a collar of lace
And a strange long chin and jawbone.

"A card for me and play your card,"
The pouting lips are scaly and hard
And a pox on the Earl o' Breadalbane.
I'll never be missed by the girls I've kissed,
I'm chained like a hawk on the rich man's wrist
And my yellow lovelocks are fallen.

"Fine's the barley and fine's the malt,"
I've broken your bread and ate your salt,
And curse the Earl o' Breadalbane.
The snowy crag and the granite cliff
Rear where I've sheltered under your roof
And I'll do a deed will appal them.

"There's my guinea and show your hand,"
Fourteen days I've been your friend;
"Aye, and ye've made a haul then."
Take your winnings and away to sleep,
Take them and go before I weep,
And fiend on the Earl o' Breadalbane!

13

"I willna hear them, I willna hear them, I willna hear the voices;
It's only the sleet and the fire o' peat and the wind and river noises.

"I willna see them, I willna see them, I willna see the shadows,
It's the ancient armour that hangs on the wall wi' the spears and
    bows and arrows.

"Surely MacIan and all his clan sleep sound in house and cabin
And I'm that's their guest should know the best that nothing is
  going to happen.

"And it's no' the sergeant and no' the lieutenant that marshall the
  men outside
But the restless cattle that move in the snow and should hae been
  put to bed.

"What did Breadalbane say to Stair and what said Stair to the
  King?
'Kill!' said Breadalbane. 'Kill!' said Stair and the King took up the
  song.

"It's only the sleet on the window pane, it whispers against the
  glass,
'Kill!' said the King to Colonel Hill and the word he had to pass.

"It's only the armour that hangs on the wall with the claymore,
  dirk and shield—
'Kill!' said the Colonel to Hamilton, and the order went to the
  field.

"Surely MacIan and all his clan sleep sound on straw or feather;
'Kill the old fox and all his cubs!' said Hamilton to the Major.

"It isna Lindsay, it isna Barber who trample the snow to filth;
Duncanson said to Captain Campbell, 'Kill if you love yourself!'

"And who do I love if I love not me, now half of the night is
  gone?"
Glenlyon strides in MacIan's hall and screams to his men, "Fall
  on!"

14

   "Out o' your bed, young John MacIan,
   Out o' your bed and awa'!
   Dinna ye hear the tramp o' boots
   In your father's house and ha'?

83

"Dinna ye hear the musket shot
That fells the big man dead,
Clamberin' into his tartan breeks
As he hustles out o' his bed?

"Up and awa', young John MacIan
Wi' the Campbell lass ye married;
The dark bonny lass, ye'll be kind wi' her
When MacDonald's dead are buried.

"Dinna ye hear the shriek that goes
Worse than the shriek o' death
As the sodgers tear at your mother's rings
Like wolves with their hungry teeth?

"Out an' awa', young John MacIan,
Chief in your father's place,
Take the word o' your serving man,
Chief o' what's left o' your race.

"Dinna ye see the form that goes
Naked and stumblin' and auld,
Your lady mother they stripped o' her clothes
To die in the dark and cauld?

"Out the door and into the snow
And owre the mountain passes;
In Appin ha' the lamp shines bright
But here there's nocht but ashes.

"Dinna ye see the blazin' torch,
Dinna ye smell the smoke,
Dinna ye hear the yells o' death
Frae the huts o' your tenant folk?

"Far frae here, young John MacIan,
Ye hid your arms frae the Campbells,
Dinna ye cry to the hills for help
Nor the river that groans and trembles.

"Here's forty MacDonalds bleed in the snow,
Ye may say their plans miscarried
For a hundred and more are awa' in the hills,
Homeless and hunted and harried.

"Then awa', awa'! though the nicht is wild
And the Coe is bloody and swollen,
For the guest in your house was Breadalbane's man
And the clan MacIan is fallen."

15

Sigh, wind in the pine;
River, weep as you flow;
Terrible things were done
Long, long ago.

In daylight golden and mild
After the night of Glencoe
They found the hand of a child
Lying upon the snow.

Lopped by the sword to the ground
Or torn by wolf or fox,
That was the snowdrop they found
Among the granite rocks.

Oh, life is fierce and wild
And the heart of the earth is stone,
And the hand of a murdered child
Will not bear thinking on.

Sigh, wind in the pine,
Cover it over with snow;
But terrible things were done
Long, long ago.

From

SUN ORCHIDS

1952

NODDING GREENHOOD

The slim green stem, the head
Bent in its green reverie;
So like the first discovery
Of what the hands could make
Or spirit dream out of rock
In the deep gully's shade . . .

All that has come to pass
Where gum-trees tower in millions
Lies in the globe of silence
The little wild orchids hold,
Lifting each hollow hood
Nine in a row from the moss.

THE GULLY

If life is here how stealthily
It moves in this green hall of rock
Where mosses flourish soft and thick
And lichens imperceptibly
In wrinkled fans and circles shape
A civilization cold as sleep
On wall of stone and fallen tree.

Only in the deep secrecy
Of bracken-fern and maidenhair
One shaft of pink is glowing here
And poised in tiny ecstasy
With all life's hunger in its look
And arm outflung for the sweet shock
The trigger-flower strikes the bee.

NATIVE INHABITANT

Red the dust and brown the rock,
Red and brown lie the leaves and bark,
And red and brown came stealing forth
An incarnation of native earth:

Bandicoot with a quivering whisker
Sits up stiff and his heart beats brisker,
Cocks his ear and twitches nose,
Then swift as a shadow off he goes;

For long ago where the leaves are brown
The blackboys laid their boomerangs down
And stood so still so many a year
They grew green leaves in place of hair.

And—now you see him and now you don't
And won't again however you hunt
For a tree that clumps on two great boots
Is a terrible sight to bandicoots;

And you will wait in a fruitless hope
Till the blackboys pick their boomerangs up
To catch the bush again like that
Off-guard in the shape of a great red rat.

A ROBIN

The vast cold silver sky
Gleams in the pool on the bluff
And the bush is grey after rain;
Little, oh, little enough

Is a morsel of wild bush robin
As long as your little finger
—A thing you could hide in your hand—
To feed the heart's great hunger

That could devour whole skies
Flaring with sunset red,
Mountains of fiery colour . . .
Bright black eyes, black head,

And one white feather in his wing,
Flashing from twig to rock,
From rock to the shallow pool
That reels with the tiny shock,

The robin darts to bathe
Breast-deep in the sky's reflection,
And all that icy trance
Breaks in most sweet destruction.

Little, oh, little enough
To fill the heart's great need,
But when he has splashed his wings
And dipped his dainty head

And spilled the drops down his back
And flown as quick as he came,
There is no need any more
To wish the mountains to flame,

For still it seems in the pool
That breast of crimson glows
And over the whole cold sky
Runs wave after wave of rose.

THE GOLDFISH POOL

The devil in the shape of a water-scorpion swam
Across the pool at sunset. Yes, beetle and gnat
And fry of the golden fishes will meet their doom
In those lean jerking arms, that horny throat,
And yet with delight I watched, and with small concern,
The rosy mirror scratched by that secret thorn:

And down where the fantail trailed his flame like a comet
And suns and scaly moons swam round and round
I looked through the eye of God for one clear moment
At naked evil spiking the luminous pond
And thought with satisfaction—or dim remorse?—
That all was well with his strange universe.

TO LIE ON THE GRASS

To lie on the grass and watch,
Amused and indifferent,
The fever that drives the ant
To nowhere that matters much;

To lie on the grass with the moths
While, spry with the thought of murder,
Goes scurrying by the spider
Speckled and muttering oaths;

To lie on the grass in a dream
Where nothing will start or stir
But the grasshopper splashing the air
With a flicker of yellow flame;

Oh, to be half asleep
In the peace of the sunlit pasture
Is to lie like a lion at leisure
Where the little kingdoms creep,

And suddenly to be confused
By a prickle of spine and hair
And a notion of eyes in the air
Indifferent and amused.

MARE AND FOAL

Tea-tree, bangally, moonlight on twist and spike:
Now, say it again, "White horse bring me good luck,"
As we used to say it in childhood; for, misty of mane,
Creamy of flank and tail, drifting like smoke
In fantastic shapes of horses from the gullies blown,
The white mare strays with her snowy foal in her wake.

This is the red road where the crow grieves
And the spider-flower lies crimson in pointed leaves,
But now in the miles of moonlight softening the ridges
There is no sound but the foal on its unshod hooves,
No colour but dusk except where the white mare trudges,
Shadow and moonshine rippling her coat like waves.

Snuffling from wide black nostrils she turns to her foal
And, scenting danger, they poise where the light is full,
Ears pricked in a creamy flare; then, warm and breathing,
The long-legged foal head-high at his mother's heel,
They pass and are gone again like white smoke wreathing.
Oh, now while the moonlight glitters from hill to hill,

What could I ask beyond the luck they brought
When, moving through trees and flowers, curving and white,
Dark-eyed, tranquil with love, shaking the mind
With all it has sought in dream or vision or thought,
The white mare came with the silver foal behind,
Immortal beauty roving a star of light?

IN THE RAIN

Bush. Mist. Rain.
The crimson salmon-gums
Drinking the runnels in
Grow leaves instead of flames;

93

And all that time when the sun
And the fires had had their will
Something was living on,
Green and grotesque and still;

For look where the raindrops shiver
And splash from the bracken frond
The green frog clasps his lover—
Emeralds broad as your hand;

As if from sandstone rock
And the blackened logs and the ash
The wand of the rain had struck
The inmost core of the bush,

A thing some spirit had made,
Sculptured, stony and cold,
With motionless thighs of jade
And foreheads crowned with gold,

And the whole wild forest's delight,
The ecstasy of the dragon,
Shown in the eyes' dark heat
Under the arching bracken—

The very heart of the bush
That, pulsing, living again,
Dares not to break the hush
Of earth and desire and rain.

THE MOTHS

Such a blaze of snow, such a smoke of sleet, such a fume of moths in
    the air
You'd think a wind of the dusk had swept the blossoming tea-trees
    bare
But the gust that blew the sunlight out and bade the thrush be silent
Has left the branches glittering white where the dark stream cuts
    the granite
And still in a whirring hush of wings the bent old tea-tree showers
Storm upon storm of snow-white moths from the midst of its cloud
    of flowers.
Bursting and foaming, spinning and gushing, secret above the
    stream,
Nothing is left of the mountains now, nothing is left of time:
Only in depths of space and night there thrusts this ragged bough
And wheeling around its cloud of flowers the galaxies swarm like
    snow.

COUNTRY OF WINTER

This time the trout are not rising at Countegany,
Not even in the weedy reaches where the current stops,
And when you climb over the ridge among the white sallys
And down the fall to the Pockets, not an insect drops,
Not a fish comes up from below, but there are only,
Looking at themselves with a shiver as a ripple laps,
The silver and the coppery trees of the wild country;
And cold among granite as a fluid shape of stone
The long pools glitter under an icy sun.

We might have seen in the dogbush this country's portent
For far in summer when guineaflower in the marsh,
Flying its golden suns, and lilies on the water
Denied that rivers are deep and rocks are harsh
And over the ragged hills and the saplings' torment
Soft lay the heat of the sun and bright its torch,
Whiter than frost was the blossom in mossy gorges;
"Snow, snow!" said the dogbush, "the hills close in
And only snow will flower in the crowding stone."

Yet there, shadowy and huge, lazy with summer,
Rising for flies or jolting the lilies about,
The rainbow swam dark crimson under the water;
And, warm while we waded, casting our flies for the trout,
When the air was blazing with noon and the insects' shimmer,
How sky and earth and water seemed opening out,
All flowers and wings and fins, all singing and colour!
What if we shattered that mirror, stained it with blood—
Where the snake uncoiled there also summer flowed.

Still in this upland country, naked in clarity,
There are two suns that talk to each other in flame,
But now there is nothing to soften their pitiless colloquy,
Not a single wing in the sky, not a ring on the stream,
And silver shudders the sun in the pool's cold purity,
Silver pours down from the sky the burning beam
And alone they commune, like gods in splendour and cruelty;
Silent at dusk the platypus sank in the deep
As if the river itself turned in its sleep.

Look, there were sally-gums, coming home late I remember,
White in a grove on the slope—how black it is now—
That stood up locked with the moonlight like lover and lover,
Such misty radiance flooding on bole and bough
They might have been trees of moonlight and danced together
Across the dim paddocks where shadows and moonrays flow.
Cold is the moon that now goes walking on the river
And each white tree crouches on the hill like a ghost,
Twisting away from the touch of stone and its taste.

All things withdraw, contract, retreat to their sources,
The snake to his hole, the wood-duck thuds to escape;
The creatures of winter come close to the lonely houses,
The dingo's shadow runs with the huddling sheep
And out with withering tea-tree and bleaching tussocks
When lamps are lit at the farms and log fires leap
Redder than fire on Andy's Flat are the foxes;
Winter comes down from the hills in a freezing mist,
Whiteness is over all and all is lost.

And how with the leaping foxes I have exulted
For all is driven, sent down in itself to endure;
And not to flourish in summer was this land moulded
But deep among snow and granite to hold its fire
Or blaze if it can before the ice has melted;
O soon at the spawning the trout will go mad with desire
Burning together, down in the dimness folded;
And fold upon fold, like the country clenching its fist,
Ridge in the river glitters to ridge in the mist.

HELMET ORCHID

Oh such a tiny colony
Set amongst all eternity
Where the great bloodwoods stand!
It is the helmet orchid
That will not lift itself
Higher than a fallen leaf
But waits intent and secret
Leaning its ear to the ground.

What could it hear but silence?
Yet where the orchid listens
Low in its purple hood
Among the trees' immensity,
Out of the depth of the world
Dark and rainy and wild
Sounding through all eternity
Silence like music flowed.

THE GREEN CENTIPEDE

Whatever lies under a stone
Lies under the stone of the world:
That day of the yellow flowers
When out of moss and shale
The cassia bushes unfurled
Their pale soft yellow stars
And lit the whole universe,
Out from the same deep source
Like some green shingly rill
From the grey stone dislodged
The big green centipede ran
Rippling down from the hill:
And fringed with silvery light,
So beautiful, not to be touched,
In its green grace had power
—Down where all rivers meet
Deep under stony ground—
To make the most gentle flower
Burn, burn in the hand.

SUNSHOWER

If he had sung a white song for every white feather
That wicked old magpie had sinned for every black
But clear he carolled on the gum-tree behind the shack
For it was a mad season of black-and-white weather
When sunshowers swept the mountains in dazzling waves
And shadow and shine seemed mixed in one tower of joy;
And loud he sang, then like some larrikin boy
Magpie and sunshower, splashing on the wet bright leaves,
Tobogganed down the old green tree together.

FLYING ANTS

Pouring straight up in their excited millions
Like smoke from the hot earth in narrow rings
The flying termites, blind in their own bright shower,
Whirl in a crystal tower not there at all:
For while the glimmering column holds them safe
To dance their delirious dance of summer and love
How frail and small it floats in the evening's brilliance:
And, striking in shafts of light that burn their wings,
Infinite space pierces the crystal wall
Where thought itself floats glinting in that tower.

THE MOPOKES

Somewhere on some wet stringybark bough there whirls night's crystal centre,
The mopoke called his mate to it and now where it spins they enter.
Cry and reply across the bush, "Mopoke" they called, "Mopoke,"
Shadow flying to shadow there and silence calling silence
As rain and midnight moved in them and trees and sandstone spoke.
Black was the night before they met and still is dark enough
—Feathers on end and glaring eye and murderous beak and talons—
Oh but how bright the centre whirls where they grapple and blaze in love.

99

THE WILD VIOLETS

O little blue-and-white violets growing wild
Between the thunder-cloud and the rage of the sea
Set your small lights in my mind as in the grass
Of those enormous cliffs all seared with salt
To mark one hour lit by my eager child
Running in a world of jewels from shells to shallows,
From rock to violet, all in one gleam of delight
Where no cliff drops its shadow and no wave follows—
Live in my mind because such moments pass
Oh like blue-and-white violets growing wild
Between the thunder-cloud and the rage of the sea.

THE FIREFLIES

But they are moving steadily, the height of a man,
Like a man among the dark trees holding a lantern
A clear small floating flame with a tinge of green,
Many small flames, all climbing the stony mountain,
Like an invisible army; but no footfalls move
Over the soft red dust, no shadow ruffles
The yellow-box-trees that the silver phalangers love;
Oh no there are no men here, there are only the fireflies,
Steadfast and radiant travelling over the spur
Where the hot earth lies heavy in dust and silence;
But indeed oh indeed some army is moving here,
Some invisible power flashing in points of brilliance
Unravelling over the earth its unearthly plans,
Uncanny to meet at night among the stones.

SHEEP COUNTRY

Woe ... Woe ... Woe!
Cries the lone black crow
In the hot blue sky.
—And with that beak
Still reeking foul
From the old cast ewe
Would you dare to pluck
The day's gold eye
From the cloud's white wool?
—Aye. If I can. Aye.

THE ABORIGINAL AXE

Hyacinth orchid, butcher-bird,
Rain on a sharp black stone:
What years like smoke and years like mist
While the butcher-bird sang in the banksia tree
And, lovely and leprous, flushed and spotted,
The hyacinth orchid bloomed and rotted,
That wet black stone has known
Since first in the scrub where the butcher-birds call
And the orchid stands up glowing and tall
Those coppery fingers let it fall
And down the track by the stony tree
The shade slipped by like a ghost.
Shaped with such care to fit the hand,
Polished and washed by the crystal shower
From stain of clay and smother of sand,
Now it lies in my own,
Warm to hold as the butcher-bird,
Cold as the rotting flower.

THE SUNFLOWERS

"Bring me a long sharp knife for we are in danger;
I see a tall man standing in the foggy corn
And his high, shadowy companions."—"But that is no stranger,
That is your company of sunflowers; and at night they turn
Their dark heads crowned with gold to the earth and the dew
So that indeed at daybreak, shrouded and silent,
Filled with a quietness such as we never knew,
They look like invaders down from another planet.
And now at the touch of light from the sun they love"—
"Give me the knife. They move."

THE FUNGUS

Leave it alone. Don't touch it! Oh, but don't touch it.
That crimson is nature's warning, those specks that blotch it
Reek with their leathery stench of corruption and poison.
And say it is only a fungus, speckled and crimson
With gaping throat and tentacles wavering out
Under a log in the sun; but then how it loves
To hide in the dark where the grass is thick and sour—
Leave it alone! For white like the egg of a snake
In its shell beside it another begins to break,
And under those crimson tentacles, down that throat,
Secret and black still gurgles the oldest ocean
Where, evil and beautiful, sluggish and blind and dumb,
Life breathes again, stretches its flesh and moves
Now like a deep-sea octopus, now like a flower,
And does not know itself which to become.

KINDRED

The rock swallows the snake,
Chilly and black as it vanishes;
In rain and moss the year
Moves in the sandstone crevices
Where like the snake itself
Earth's darkest impulses brood.
Long stems, sharp leaves awake—
O look where the wet moss flourishes
Tall crimson orchids appear,
Snake-headed, with darting tongue,
Now this way striking, now that,
As if indeed they had sprung
From the black snake's rotting side
Under the sandstone shelf
To spill on the green air
Their dewdrops of dark thought
Like venom and like blood.

FLOWER OF WINTER

Surely because it is winter and westerlies rush
From icy highlands beating the branches down
Travail must shape some pure white thought in the bush
Where leaf and bark lie brown on the dream of stone
And only the flannel-flowers, numb as the earth, endure
The season of death on one huge rocky spur.

Surely some thought—but colder over its stones
Scurries the creek to drop in the dusk of the gorge,
Wilder rushes the wind . . . And there it stands
Frail as a thought indeed on the mind's dark verge,
Fringed with faint purple out of the warmth below,
The ghostly caladenia whiter than snow.

TONGUE ORCHID

Moth or flower, flower or moth,
Neither moth nor flower but both
Fly in one sweet crystal flesh
Where the white tongue-orchids break
Dazzling from the old grey rock.

Day's clear blue and sunlight dappling
Apple-gum and she-oak sapling,
Like long fine wings the petals flash;
But O from what grey depths of time
These flowers fly in their white dream.

MAHONY'S MOUNTAIN

If there's a fox, he said, I'll whistle the beggar;
And shrill the counterfeit cry of the rabbit's pain
Rang out in the misty clearing; so soon to be lost
In the stony spurs and candlebarks darker and huger
Where Mahony's mountain towers in drifts of rain.
No sharp wild face out of burrow or hollow stump,
No rustle shaking the raindrops from rushes or flowers
—Greenhood and bulbine lily lighting the swamp—
Nothing but bush and silence; so on and up
Tramping through moss where so many violets cluster
You cannot help but crush them; and still more steep
The sheep-track winds through the dripping leaves and the rocks,
And still no fox, no bandicoot's tiny fluster,
No flurry of green rosellas flashing past,
Nothing but the huge grey silence, the trees and—look,
There where the mountain breaks on its granite peak,
The doubletail orchid, O like some fairytale fox,
Whistled from earth by a wilder call than ours,
Pricks up its yellow ears and stares through the mist.

TERRA AUSTRALIS

1

Captain Quiros and Mr William Lane,
Sailing some highway shunned by trading traffic
Where in the world's skull like a moonlit brain
Flashing and crinkling rolls the vast Pacific,

Approached each other zigzag, in confusion,
Lane from the west, the Spaniard from the east,
Their flickering canvas breaking the horizon
That shuts the dead off in a wall of mist.

"Three hundred years since I set out from Lima
And off Espiritu Santo lay down and wept
Because no faith in men, no truth in islands
And still unfound the shining continent slept;

"And swore upon the Cross to come again
Though fever, thirst and mutiny stalked the seas
And poison spiders spun their webs in Spain,
And did return, and sailed three centuries,

"Staring to see the golden headlands wade
And saw no sun, no land, but this wide circle
Where moonlight clots the waves with coils of weed
And hangs like silver moss on sail and tackle,

"Until I thought to trudge till time was done
With all except my purpose run to waste;
And now upon this ocean of the moon,
A shape, a shade, a ship, and from the west!"

2

"What ship?" "The *Royal Tar*!" "And whither bent?"
"I seek the new Australia." "I, too, stranger;
Terra Australis, the great continent
That I have sought three centuries and longer;

"And westward still it lies, God knows how far,
Like a great golden cloud, unknown, untouched,
Where men shall walk at last like spirits of fire
No more by oppression chained, by sin besmirched."

"Westward there lies a desert where the crow
Feeds upon poor men's hearts and picks their eyes;
Eastward we flee from all that wrath and woe
And Paraguay shall yet be Paradise."

"Eastward," said Quiros, as *San Pedro* rolled,
High-pooped and round in the belly like a barrel,
"Men tear each other's entrails out for gold;
And even here I find that men will quarrel."

"If you are Captain Quiros you are dead."
"The report has reached me; so is William Lane."
The dark ships rocked together in the weed
And Quiros stroked the beard upon his chin:

"We two have run this ocean through a sieve
And though our death is scarce to be believed
Seagulls and flying-fish were all it gave
And it may be we both have been deceived."

3

"Alas, alas, I do remember now;
In Paradise I built a house of mud
And there were fools who could not milk a cow
And idle men who would not though they could.

"There were two hundred brothers sailed this ocean
To build a New Australia in the east
And trifles of money caused the first commotion
And one small cask of liquor caused the last.

"Some had strange insects bite them, some had lust,
For wifeless men will turn to native women,
Yet who could think a world would fall in dust
And old age dream of smoke and blood and cannon

"Because three men got drunk?" "With Indian blood
And Spanish hate that jungle reeked to Heaven;
And yet I too came once, or thought I did,
To Terra Australis, my dear western haven,

"And broke my gallows up in scorn of violence,
Gave land and honours, each man had his wish,
Flew saints upon the rigging, played the clarions:
Yet many there were poisoned by a fish

"And more by doubt; and so deserted Torres
And sailed, my seamen's prisoner, back to Spain."
There was a certain likeness in the stories
And Captain Quiros stared at William Lane.

4

Then "Hoist the mainsail!" both the voyagers cried,
Recoiling each from each as from the devil;
"How do we know that we are truly dead
Or that the tales we tell may not be fable?

"Surely I only dreamed that one small bottle
Could blow up New Australia like a bomb?
A mutinous pilot I forebore to throttle
From Terra Australis send me demented home?

"The devil throws me up this Captain Quiros,
This William Lane, a phantom not yet born,
This Captain Quiros dead three hundred years,
To tempt me to disaster for his scorn—

"As if a blast of bony breath could wither
The trees and fountains shining in my mind,
Some traveller's tale, puffed out in moonlit weather,
Divert me from the land that I must find!

"Somewhere on earth that land of love and faith
In Labour's hands—the Virgin's—must exist,
And cannot lie behind, for there is death,
So where but in the west—but in the east?"

At that the sea of light began to dance
And plunged in sparkling brine each giddy brain;
The wind from Heaven blew both ways at once
And west went Captain Quiros, east went Lane.

From WORSLEY ENCHANTED

2

He travels into the country of his dream.

White, said Worsley, and glistening, the ridgy plain
Of sea-water, frozen; being a known substance,
Though changed. As changes the frozen brain.
The sky, too, uncertain. At a little distance
A violet mist arises, fume of the frost,
Soon turned to gold to hide the killing of the ship,
The water black in her hold when her timbers burst,
Her body, black on the ice, raised twisting up
On the marching floes, then dropped and trampled; crushed.
There were men and dogs on the ice, a litter of gear,
But where, what place in the world, when the dead sea flushed
With the glare of five suns in the sky, five wheels of fire
Spinning in the streams of crimson, where the winter moon
In rushing silver swept the perpetual night,
And gentle as dream in wavering rose and green
In an abstract beauty, a kind of flowering of light,
The aurora flowed its colours across the mind?
We longed very much to stand on solid land.

True there were days of blue and rime in the sun,
We laughed like men; and then above the horizon,
Floating in light, a violet and creamy line,
The ice-pack swam in the heavens, wavy and frozen,
And someone who stood, say, where we began our drift,
At the point in the moving ice where the ship went down,
Would see us too with the golden bergs that lift
And shift in the air in the blue Antarctic noon,
Stumbling in frozen colour. I saw in that sky,
Huge, dark, Shackleton; the tall man striding
Through the lights that flash like mathematics at play,
Through mountains floating in air and icebergs flying,
In a land beyond that wall of ice or glass
Through which men have seen at times glowing shadows.
Is it the natural world through which we pass
Or the supernatural? In the cold shallows and hollows
I have seen the two as one, and gripped with my hand
The wood of a boat, and longed for solid land.

3

*He meditates on the nine Emperor penguins which, on the day the
Endurance was destroyed by the pack-ice, appeared from a crack in
the ice and uttered wailing cries, "quite unlike any we had heard
before", that sounded like a dirge for the ship.*

Oh, there was broken wood,
There were weeds of iron and rope,
The log that was bigger than a tree
Crashed on the frozen sea
And the tall dark penguins stood
And stared at the ice without hope,
Said the nine Emperor penguins.

And these were a race of birds
Majestic, beyond belief;
There where the gold mist hung
They spoke in a foreign tongue,
Loud, sharp, excited words,
They rocked and shook with grief,
Said the nine Emperor penguins.

Bowing we stepped up close,
Our numbers making us brave,
But grinding like frozen thunder
Across the black seas under
Jagged reared up the floes
And crushed that ship in her grave,
Said the nine Emperor penguins.

Oh, it was strange, it was proud,
It was the worst of things,
In the mist and the darkening clouds
Something had happened to our gods
And we were alone and afraid
Who trod the ice like kings
Said the nine Emperor penguins.

We knew what the blue sea hid,
Sea-leopard and killer whale;
There was no day beneath
The sun but we thought of death
And shook off the shadow and slid
To the comber's foam and its fall,
Said the nine Emperor penguins.

But now we have learned a truth
Not easy to shake from the feather
For we know what the blue sky hides,
Penguins that stride like gods,
And under the killer's tooth
Lie gods and birds together,
Said the nine Emperor penguins.

Nobody knows where they went,
They came from the sky and are gone
But we remember a ship
Crushed in the ice-floes' grip,
The black thing broken and rent,
And we shudder with cold in the sun,
Said the nine Emperor penguins.

4

*He watches the men on Elephant Island after their six months'
drift on an ice-floe.*

But these men picked up pebbles
Wet from the sea and cold
And cradled them in their hands
As if they were coins of gold;
As if they had ended their troubles
On those lost frozen sands.

As if out of shells on the shore
Human voices would speak,
As if the crag was a house
And the kind wind would cook
On the thin and hungry fire
Gobbets of stone and ice.

Well might the seagulls screech
As reeling upon the sand
Like madmen and like devils
That starving, ragged band
Danced on the strip of beach
Their brief and scarecrow revels.

5

He hears Crean singing at the tiller of the James Caird, *when, with the singer, Shackleton, and three other men, he is voyaging in the ship's boat to South Georgia to bring help to the men on Elephant Island.*

"Nine hundred stormy miles"
The wet wind sang to Crean,
And Crean sang at the tiller
"The Wearin' o' the Green".

"South Georgia's far away
And Ireland's further yet,
And black are the night and the sea
For a man to be singing at."

6

He hears, as the sixteen days' voyage progresses, the undersong of that "flat, dreary but somehow heartening tune".

It's cold, says Crean at the tiller,
And dim in my mind I hear
The sound of a keel on shingle
And surf on a faraway beach
Where ice and pebbles mingle
And, thin for a moment, a cheer
Dying on crags out of reach.

Grey water, grey weather,
Sang Crean at the tiller,
The snowflake's cold feather,
The hiss of the foam;
Four days of grey weather
For whale and for killer
And I have come home.

Oh grey-green abysses of water
Oh mountains that fall on the deck,
Deep in the trough of a comber
Then high, sang Crean, in the sky
Matting I saw and timber;
Somebody's dead in a wreck,
Alive in the storm am I.

My friend the porpoise is coming
To roll and to plunge and to tunnel
Black where the blue seas are gleaming,
Sang Crean in the sunny *James Caird*;
So hang up my socks till they're steaming,
Roll off the ice in a runnel,
Wring out the salt from my beard.

Morning and evening falling,
Crean sang at the tiller,
And stones and men rolling
Gather no kindly moss
But the spray from the wind howling
As low on the long grey roller
Skims the great albatross.

Twelve days of endless combers
Roll, said Crean, in my song,
A weary voyage for roamers
Almost as tired as the dead
Fumbling in broken murmurs
For words that dry on the tongue
Or fade in the fog ahead.

Oh cool ice, sweet snow,
Oh spray that pretends to be rain,
Oh brooks that sing as you flow
Blot yourselves out of my thirst,
Sang Crean dogged and slow;
A man with a bearded grin
Licking his lips in the mist.

Crean sang in the storm
The loneliest song on earth
Of how the heart was warm
And yet a man might come
With his hand on the tiller firm
To his last setting-forth
Gaunt, frozen and dumb.

10

Worsley in the hurricane

Not the hunger not the thirst,
All this world's a world accursed;
Since the day we lost the *Endurance*
Nothing's come but came like nonsense;
Black she lay with her frosty mast,
Here's their dirtiest trick at last.
Not the storm, the devil take it,
I can bale it out in a bucket,
But on what fool's errand bent
To cross the Antarctic continent
Came I here to the South at all?
Not the shrieking knife of the gale
Slashing off the comber's crest,
Not the land we found and lost,
But here the whole world stands on its head
Crazy alive and crazy dead.
Stand up straight or upside-down,
Die in your bed or swim and drown
But why and in what shadow play
Fights a man till break of day
Where the hurricane that raves
Where the midnight, where the waves
Are shadows of some vaster doom
Shaking the spirit, seen in dream?

15

They have the impression that a fourth man is travelling with them.

This man is nothing, invisible,
This man is ghostly, impossible,
Nobody following us, nobody
Keeping us silent company.
Casting no shadow he follows
Our long black following shadows.

"Some seaman's ghost perhaps?
Some traveller from the crevasses?"
In the mountains there are no ships,
And this way no traveller passes.
He is not here but he watches us,
Checked on the edge of the precipice.

"Creatures of tempests and mists?"
God help them if they go
Wandering these white wastes
While centuries sink in snow.
This is no country for men,
A land like the back of the moon.

"I cannot touch him nor see,
I cannot speak to the air."
Only we know we are three
And a fourth man is moving here:
On his own purposes bent,
Grave and indifferent.

All night and all day and all night
In the mountainous land without rest,
And the trudging of heavy feet,
The fingers of fog on the crest:
He gives no direction, no warning,
He is light in the sunlight burning.

115

All things flower out of nothing:
Here nothing itself is moving;
For this man is nothing, intangible,
Yet he is with us, unchangeable,
Travelling the snowfields, somebody,
Keeping us silent company.

16

Crean and Worsley fall into the sleep of exhaustion.

At the foot of the final spur we lay in the snow,
The light drift whitening our clothes. The last I saw
Was Shackleton, hunched and immense, the moon on his brow
Lighting the eagle's mouth and the bearded face.
The glittering planet swung in the circle of space.
Shackleton woke us: "I was not alone while I watched
But if I had fallen asleep he would not have spoken
Nor laid on mortal flesh the touch of immortal;
Pity is in their mind, their actions pitiless."
These words were spoken at dawn at the end of the world.
The bundles of death that had slept in the snow uncurled,
A gap of colour showed where the peaks were broken
And there, far down, with a grey and misty glimmer
Lay Stromness Bay, and safety, and Husvik Harbour.

From

THE BIRDSVILLE TRACK

1955

WOMBAT

Ha there! old pig, old bear, old bristly and gingery
Wombat out of the red earth peering gingerly
Was there some thud of foot in the mist and the silence
That stiffens whisker and ear in sound's fierce absence,
Some smell means man?
I see the dewdrop trembling upon the rushes,
All else is the mist's now, river and rocks and ridges.
Poor lump of movable clay, snuffling and blinking,
Too thick in the head to know what thumps in your thinking,
Rears in the rain—
Be easy, old tree-root's companion; down there where your burrow
Dips in its yellow shadow, deep in the hollow,
We have one mother, good brother; it is Her laughter
That sends you now snorting and plunging like red flood-water
To earth again.

CROW'S NEST

Never since the stringybarks stiffened to telegraph poles
And froze their flowers in porcelain has a crow been known
To nest in a tree at Crow's Nest. The traffic rolls
Blindly on birds' and blackfellows' bones in the stone
And harsh and far, oh harsh and far cry the crows
To the first man climbing in the heat through the rocky forest.
Nevertheless, where the tramlines cross and recross
To make a new nest of steel for fruit-shop and florist
And neon signs glare as red as any bushfire,
Fifteen land-agents picking the eyes of the land,
Twenty car-salesmen waiting to fly at the buyer,
Five roads leaping to kill at the traffic-cop's hand
And ten glossy undertakers eager to deal with the rest
Prove there are crows enough still if you look at Crow's Nest.

THE FINCHES

Flit flit flit they cry in their bright voices
Showering upon the lawn, the firetail finches
Blowing from nowhere like broken leaves and berries
From some far briar-bush that the wind harries
In a flurry of soft green bodies, red beak and tail;
And flit they do when they have picked what they wanted,
Miles through the mountains again, so small, so undaunted,
As if they can see some sweet and sheltering briar
Formed of their own green flight and tips of fire
Where finches are safe wherever they blow with the gale.

CHRISTMAS BELLS

See them, the wild children
Running in their straight frocks
Of boldest orange and vermilion
All day in the sandstone rocks;

Where, sliding his crimson scales,
The black snake rustles and flows
Down the dry waterfalls
And smoky the blue wind blows,

Heady and hot from the hollow,
Telling what robe of fear
Scarlet and flaring yellow
The summer forest will wear.

"My children will never behave
They have the sun's hot flesh,"
Cries the old mother in her cave;
"There on their long bare legs

"In the sun, in the smoke, in the threat,
Out from the cool stone shelves,
They dance all day in the heat
Like little bushfires themselves."

FOXES

I saw a fine fox, I saw a fine fox,
He held up a rabbit in his mouth
And that was at Duckmaloi.
There were granite rocks
In the tumbled hills
And willows all gold
And hot red berries
In the wild-briar's teeth.

Oh who was his double, the other fine fox
Who leapt from my heart where he smoulders?
They met that morning in joy.
There were huge grey rocks
Very round, very old,
And the little red bells
Of the berries all rang
As the fox ran away on the boulders.

MOSQUITO ORCHID

Such infinitesimal things,
Mosquito orchids flying
Low where the grass-tree parts
And winter's sun lies dying
In a flash of green and bronze
On the dead beetle's wings
Among the broken stones.

Such infinitesimal things
And yet so many, so many,
Little green leaves like hearts,
Bright wings and red antennae
All swarming into the cold,
It seems the whole hillside stings
And glints from the grey leaf-mould.

CRAB AND CICADA

Some flying-fish then? Some green fantastic lobster?
But never in wave or crevice was seen such a monster.
Why then, old claw of the ocean, blood-red and purple,
Gripping so rare a banquet of splendour and peril
Where, warily, tip of your nipper to wing's fine shoulder,
You crouch on the sunny rock with the big cicada
Who fell down dazed and singing from the shining air—
That's the green earth you clutch: and ages and ages
Ago it climbed the cliff where no wave reaches
And towered with the powers that strike from the air, old pirate.
See, even this green innocent, beating and desperate,
Stares with its eyes like suns to burn and startle;
"Chir! Chir!" it says with its hard rocky rattle
And dine you may, but you may well beware.

BRINDABELLA

Once on a silver and green day, rich to remember,
When thick over sky and gully rolled winter's grey wave
And one lost magpie was straying on Brindabella
I heard the mountain talking in a tall green cave
Between the pillars of the trees and the moss below:
It made no sound but talked to itself in snow.

All the white words were falling through the timber
Down from the old grey thought to the flesh of rock
And some were of silence and patience, and spring after winter,
Tidings for leaves to catch and roots to soak,
And most were of being the earth and floating in space
Alone with its weather through all the time there is.

Then it was, struck with wonder at this soliloquy,
The magpie lifting his beak by the frozen fern
Sent out one ray of a carol, softened and silvery,
Strange through the trees as sunlight's pale return,
Then cocked his black head and listened, hunched from the cold,
Watching that white whisper fill his green world.

THE BROWN SNAKE

I walked to the green gum-tree
Because the day was hot;
A snake could be anywhere
But that time I forgot.

The Duckmaloi lazed through the valley
In amber pools like tea
From some old fossicker's billy,
And I walked under the tree.

Blue summer smoked on Bindo,
It lapped me warm in its waves,
And when that snake hissed up
Under the shower of leaves

Huge, high as my waist,
Rearing with lightning's tongue,
So brown with heat like the fallen
Dry sticks it hid among,

I thought the earth itself
Under the green gum-tree,
All in the sweet of summer
Reached out to strike at me.

THE LAST OF SNOW

It is the last of the snow
Under a bush on the heath
Like a little white calf forgotten
While sunlight bares its teeth;

And still where Bullock's Head Creek
Spills down to the Eucumbene
And the granite highlands sprawl
Without one shoot of green,

That broken briar, that heath
Flattened and crushed and tramped
Show as if in vast shadows
The place where the cattle camped,

Drowsing all winter through
In a dream with their mild eyes full
Of blizzard and flying starlight,
The cow lying down by the bull.

And they pressed their mighty forms
On the rough green rug below,
And they swayed their horns of ice:
The wild white cattle of snow.

Little white calf, stand up
And follow the wild mob
Far over Bullock's Head Creek,
Over Kiandra's top.

SPIDER-GUMS

Where winter's snow and crashing rains
Have forced the snow-gums to their knees,
High in the sky on Kelly's Plains
These frail and delicate spider-trees:

As though some pigtailed fossicker here
Now bleached as quartz on Dead Man Range
Had drawn a Chinese sketch on air
To speak for him when all should change;

Or high from where the Murrumbidgee's
Tussocky rapids flash and race
A flying swarm of water-midges
Hangs in a mist of light and lace.

As though through summer's huge hot noon
Lost drifts of winter linger still
And twenty flakes of snow are blown
All dark against the granite hill;

Or light winds silvery with frost
Have breathed upon the sky's blue glass
To make a tree that seems half ghost
And melts into the russet grass.

As though in earth's deep dream of stone
Some leafy thought was taking form
And fled before the dream was done,
Half-finished out to sun and storm;

Or some tall tree not there at all
Has flecked the sunlight with its shadow
And shadows' shadows glide and fall
Dark green upon air's crystal hollow;

As though, as though—but now I see
The white clouds covering the blue,
A chill breeze beating on the tree
That hardly shakes as it goes through,

And know how earth took deepest thought
In this cold kingdom of the winter
To make some shape of grace to float
Secure while snow-gums crack and splinter,

And made this phantom tree at last,
A thing more air than leaf or bough,
That slips clean through the killing blast
And dances clear from all the snow.

MURRUMBIDGEE

Water with a dark-green dorsal-fin
Darting where black-spinners spin

Under the tussocks in the high red rocky
Windswept kangaroo-grass country;

Water waving a lazy tail
In blue pools dreaming in granite shale

Where the spider-gums reflected lie
Like a ruffle of wind across the sky:

Water flashing like a fish in the sun
Where the glittering rapid strikes on stone—

Oh the Murrumbidgee comes leaping out
High on Kelly's like a silver trout:

And who'd have thought that it could grow
Such a monster so soon below

With too much knowledge and too much food
Of crops and cattle drowned in flood

And rolling through the Monaro lie
Like a great cod at Gundagai

That, all its youth forgotten, wallows
Brooding and gross beneath the willows

And hopes next time the rains come down
That it can swallow the whole town.

THE NIGHT OF THE MOTHS

The giant moths like sparrows! So many drowned
On the stony mountain struggling out of the ground,
So many battered from the air by the wind and the storm
Where the black rain beats on Bindo; yet still they swarm
From the tunnel in the clay, from the dark wet undergrowth,
Through the night and the trees, great whirring moth by moth.

The midnight hides their long clear rainy wings,
Their bodies of gold; blindly the black earth flings
Its passion of blind black life to meet the rain;
And one with the storm, with the trees as they shudder and strain,
One with the mountain shambling in night and stone,
Up the dark ridge they fly, and they are gone.

EVERLASTING

So here you are, my small hot friend,
Lighting the Badja's granite bend
While high and clear the thrushes call
Like flashing spray above the fall:
A flower, a clock, an everlasting
Growing in the driftwood heap and casting
Your scrap of yellow light on stone
As if you thought by this wild river
You'd pass for your great lord the sun
Who shines up there like some big daisy
And pours his light indeed for ever
Through the tall gums and down the valley.

And it is true, my beaming midget:
Heaven is far, but you shall bridge it
For ray by ray and flame by flame
Together here you lit the stream
Rustling your stiff petals open
Out of the mist that dawn should happen,
Widening now for noon's high hour;
And who could doubt while so you rhyme,
Flower to sun and sun to flower,
That earth and heaven chime as one
And clear and golden is the time
All the space from here to the sun.

CICADA SONG

Sumer is icumen in,
Loud sing cicada!
Bulljo nippeth, black snake slippeth
Sun biteth harder.

Treetops ring with peals of light
(Merry sing Greengrocer!)
Red bark cracketh, blue smoke tracketh,
Bushfire stealeth closer.
Sing cicada!

Black Prince with his ruby eyes
Stareth at the season;
Doubledrummer drunk with summer
Shrilleth past all reason.

Sing Floury Baker, Yellow Monday,
Bright as sun on bough;
Sing cicada, sing cicada,
Sing cicada now.

THE SNOW-GUM

It is the snow-gum silently,
In noon's blue and the silvery
Flowering of light on snow,
Performing its slow miracle
Where upon drift and icicle
Perfect lies its shadow.

Leaf upon leaf's fidelity,
The creamy trunk's solidity,
The full-grown curve of the crown,
It is the tree's perfection
Now shown in clear reflection
Like flakes of soft grey stone.

Out of the granite's eternity,
Out of the winters' long enmity,
Something is done on the snow;
And the silver light like ecstasy
Flows where the green tree perfectly
Curves to its perfect shadow.

From THE BIRDSVILLE TRACK

1. *The Fierce Country*

Three hundred miles to Birdsville from Marree
Man makes his mark across a fierce country
That has no flower but the whitening bone and skull
Of long-dead cattle, no word but "I will kill".

Here the world ends in a shield of purple stone
Naked in its long war against the sun;
The white stones flash, the red stones leap with fire:
It wants no interlopers to come here.

Whatever it is that speaks through softer earth
Still tries to stammer indeed its broken phrases;
Between some crack in the stone mosaic brings forth
Yellow and white like suns the papery daisies;

The cassia drinks the sky in its gold cup,
Straggling on sandhills the dwarf wild-hops lift up
Their tufts of crimson flame; and the first hot wind
Blows out the suns and smothers the flames in sand.

And man too like the earth in the good season
When the Diamantina floods the whole horizon
And the cattle grow fat on wildflowers says his proud word:
Gathers the stones and builds four-square and hard:

Where the mirage still watches with glittering eyes
The ruins of his homestead crumble on the iron rise.
Dust on the waterless plains blows over his track,
The sun glares down on the stones and the stones glare back.

2. *Marree*

Oh the corrugated-iron town
In the corrugated-iron air
Where the shimmering heat-waves glare
To the red-hot iron plain
And the steel mirage beyond:

The blackfellow's squalid shanty
Of rags and bags and tins,
The bright-red dresses of the gins
Flowering in that hot country
Like lilies in the dust's soft pond:

The camels' bones and the bullocks',
The fierce red acre of death
Where the Afghan groans beneath
His monstrous concrete blankets
That peel in the heat like rind:

Where life if it hopes to breathe
Must crawl in the shade of a stone
Like snake and scorpion:
All tastes like dust in the mouth,
All strikes like iron in the mind.

3. *The Nameless*

Glint of pebbles in the sun,
Dark red and shining white.
Snug in their iron railings
That shut the desert out
While marble angels weep
Shimmering tears of heat
The lucky dead men keep
Their names alive on a stone
With texts of pious hope
And no recorded failings.

But each in his glinting mound
Of pebbles raked in a heap,
Without one mark to show
There is a man below
Except that long low shape,
Lie the nameless ones;
And cook like bread in an oven.

In the pubs, on the plains,
In the sun's white blink,
Some died of too much drink
And some of not enough;
And all may be in heaven.
But gone, gone out of mind.
A dead man should have a name.

What's a bare heap of stones
For pity or for love,
For praise or blame or fame?

5. *Afghan*

Mopping his coppery forehead under his turban,
Old Bejah in baggy trousers, bearded, immense:
"Oh ya, oh ya, the young man dead in the sands,
I dig with my hands, I find him, and fifty yards further
The other, both dead, so young; no water, no water."
The gestures, the voice, all larger and wilder than human,
Some whirlwind out of the desert. "Two days in the sun,
Done when I sight the camp. I shoot off my gun
And Larry Wells he carry me over his shoulder;
Looking for water out there; oh ya, no water."
Old camel-driver, explorer, the giant Afghan
Who steered his life by compass and by Koran,
"Oh ya, believe in God; young man no care;
God save, God help; oh ya, need help out there!"
And fondled his box of brass and kissed his book
So passionately, with such a lover's look,
He whirled in deserts still, too wild for human.

9. *The Brumby*

Two dingoes and a brumby:
The tawny dog and the white bitch
And the stallion dead from thirst.
When they had ate and drunk their fill
They loped into the blazing west,
The tawny dog and the white bitch
By stony flat and sandy hill
To where they lay in light's own lair
Of burning stone and white-hot air;
Two dingoes quit the brumby.
And stark and stiff when they had gone
Like bitch of light and dog of flame
The black horse lay and kicked the sun
Whence all this evil came.

132

10. *The Humorists*

The red cow died and the Hereford bull,
Two figures more to cancel:
Dan Corcoran took a bullock's skull
And wrote on it with a pencil:
"Here I lie on the Birdsville Track
Driven to death by Scotty Mac."
Scotty Mac laughed fit to kill,
Saw it six months later;
Took another and tried his skill:
"Here I lie like an old tin can
Kicked down the Track by droving Dan"—
Thus drover joked with drover.
Whether the bullocks laughed as well
Nobody knows or cares;
But what they wrote on a bullock's skull
A bullock could write on theirs.

11. *Ruins*

Two golden butterflies mating over the ruins
Of the iron house that is nowhere's dark dead centre
Stark on the rise in the huge hot circle of the plains
All doors and windows gaping for the wind to enter—
Lord, Lord they think that nowhere is all the world
And, so they can dance their golden dance of love,
One hot blue day in the desert more than enough.

And in that same dark house when her husband perished
The woman, they say, lived on so long alone
With what she could think and the household things she
  cherished,
Staring at that vast island of purple stone
Without one break until the mirage unfurled
Its ocean of steel, it tore a great gap in her mind
Harsh as the loose sheet of iron that bangs in the wind.

12. *The Mules*

Having no foal of their own those two mad mules
Ran aching over the red stone plain for miles
And where the thorn-bush softened the hot blue air
With shade and prickly flowers they found the mare
And bared their teeth and took her foal for their own.
Oh they were mad and happy those two dark mules,
They ran at the mother wild with their flying heels,
Their long ears wagged with love as they nuzzled her colt,
Brooding like a cloud above it, not knowing their fault:
They had no milk to give suck and it died on the stone.

13. *Place Names*

Ethadinna, Mira Mitta,
Mulka, Mungerannie—
Dark shadows blown
With the dust away,
Far from our day
Far out of time,
Fill the land with water.
Where the blue sky flames
On the bare red stone,
Dulkaninna, Koperamanna,
Ooroowilanie, Kilalpaninna—
Only the names
In the land remain
Like a dark well
Like the chime of a bell.

14. *Sombrero*

In a cowboy hat and a dark-green shirt,
Lithe on a piebald pony,
The blackfellow rode through the coolabah trees
Where the creek was dry and stony.

Here's fifty horses from Pandie Pandie
To drove to far Marree
But before I start on the track again
I'll boil up a billy of tea.

Oh he was dark as the gibber stones
And took things just as easy
And a white smile danced on his purple lips
Like an everlasting daisy.

The horses strayed on the saltbush plain
And he went galloping after,
The green shirt flew through the coolabah trees
Like budgerigars to water.

And then what need had he to sigh
For old men under the gibbers
When he was free as the winds that blow
Along the old dry rivers?

He had the lubras' hot wild eyes,
His green shirt and sombrero,
He rode the plains on a piebald horse
And he was his own hero.

15. *Outlaw*

What if the country bred no more
Than some Ned Kelly or Ben Hall
And with the outlaw's hate and fear
That lion-coloured dingo runs
Uneasy by the lignum bush
Waiting the shot, the pain, the fall,
The red calf paid for to the full—

Still in this burning place of stones
While there is none more fierce than he,
More cruel and cunning, wild and free,
More self-sufficient, self-secure
On wastes of stone and sun and sand,
I saw him in that murderous hush
The lion of his lean land.

17. *Blazes Well*

And when they came to Blazes Well
The sides had fallen in,
The hot wind blew on the high windmill
And the bent vane would not spin.

There was no water on that plain
But fire in stone and air
Licking the cattle bones again
That dingoes had picked bare.

And from that well of empty hope
From iron tower and spoke
The silly crying galahs flew up
Like red flame and like smoke.

136

18. *Mirage*

Not that he'd go as some indeed would run
Stumbling across the waste of hot red stone
Where like some crystal snake the heat-haze writhes
To drink that water that had not water's look
(Oh gentle smile of the creek where green grass flourished)
But rather was steel flame and purple smoke
Towering upon the horizon: some raw new-chum
Who soon enough would be pulling off his clothes
And raving in crazy circles till he perished
While the water that was not water flowed over him.

Not that for him! Only it had a way
Of seeming to creep through the saltbush greenish and grey,
You could not see for the bushes where it ended,
Into what inlet now that silver flood—
Oh did not, could not creep, and was not water
But the glitter of sun on stone; and if it moved,
Why, keeping its place the enormous mirror shone
East, west and north with trees and hills suspended,
And steadfast behind no doubt it followed after
If you turned to look . . . but water was on, was on.

And indeed when it thrust some long hot steely tongue,
Between the sandhills where the red clouds hung,
Into that shallow basin was once a lake
It had some look of water; those green reflections
In long miraculous pools still left from the rain
Six months ago; why, water in all directions,
On the track, on the stones, on the sandhills, so near you could
    touch.
And touch that molten steel! As well mistake
That cloud of eaglehawks wheeling above the plain
For seagulls, seagulls—where the white foam on the beach . . .

137

Never that he'd plunge—but they came close that lot,
And it was quiet now and it was hot.
There were one hundred seagulls flying inland
Barred gold and black, all watching the hard ground,
They had their eye on something; but so had he,
It welled up high and glittered all around.
And was no more, no more than that great tide
Where first he saw the cloud become an island
And many an island green with many a tree
Now high in air as still came on the flood.

You had to watch it for its trick of sneaking
Between the bushes there while you weren't looking
Or while you were; or jumping clean ten miles
In silver discs that flashed across the stones
And vanished or did not; or swelling, mounting
In such a wave that he must run at once.
Why it could come like that—but it was coming,
That rill of silver trickling down the hills,
But more but more, too many streams for counting,
Oh everywhere in one great wave was looming—

He splashed in shallow water to his knees.
Oh yet might make that island and those trees,
Climb high in air if not too high for climbing,
And he could drink at last in that great flood—
But had not water's coolness, water's taste,
O seared the tongue, ran fire through all his blood.
The hawks dropped down to watch him as he drank.
Some lost far voice cried "No!" but he was swimming
And round and round, could no way sight the coast,
Until the bright flame took him and he sank.

19. *Night Camp*

Sleep, traveller, under the thorn on the stones.
Somewhere on earth a man must lie down in trust
And though behind you, cold as it breathes on your hand,
Thudding like surf through the desert, foaming with dust,
Rushes the wind that moves the hills of sand,
What need of more than a bush to turn the gale?
Sleep, all's well.
Look where the dusty blossoms shake on the thorn
Over your head, like motes in a shaft of the moon
Climbing and falling, fluttering their wings now come
Tiny white moths that call this desert home.

21. *The Seaweeds*

Not in our time but lost in a long dream
Grey and green and silver the saltbush floats
Its glistening leaves and bubbles between the pebbles,
The waterbush drips on the sand its purple stain.
When the old ocean fell through a hole in time
And the great monsters choked with sand in their throats
Everything perished, everything changed into fables,
The crow and the sun stare down on the bare stone plain:
Only the seaweeds, cool in each secret cell,
Saltbush and waterbush dream in the long green swell.

25. *The Branding Fire*

The dust, the smoke and the yellow fire on
The red plain heating the branding-iron,
As though the sun's long white-hot blast
Had struck the stones to flame at last.
And where the stockmen bronze and hard
Roll their smokes in the high stockyard
And watch that wild young bull break loose
Defiant from the calves and cows,
And bellowing with rage and pain
Run mad across the vast hot plain
With tail out stiff and tossing horns,
Kicking the stones up when he turns
To meet the blackboy cantering after,
Like smouldering coals I hear their laughter;
Like man's own will I see that fire,
Who stamps the stones with his desire,
Who herds his beasts and burns his brand
Like red-hot iron on this red land.

From

RUTHERFORD

1962

PROFESSOR PICCARD

Some said it was a shooting star,
Some said it was a pheasant;
It was the most surprising thing
To villager and peasant.

To see it floating and shining there
Over the alps of snow—
Some said it was a bubble of air,
The others they said no;

It could not be just snow or cloud
Or any such phenomenon,
It could not be a water spout,
At least it was no common one

For they could see a shape inside
That stood too straight and tall
To be a weed or fish caught up—
If it was there at all.

Some said it was a man in a bottle,
But they had drunk too well;
Some said it was a shining spirit
Released from heaven or hell;

Some said it was a thing from Mars
And some the man in the moon;
And some said it was Professor Piccard
Ascending in his balloon.

His bright blue eyes were filled with heaven,
His hair like wisps of cloud,
And straight like an exclamation mark
In the high noon he stood.

And up and up to the stratosphere,
Always sublimely vertical,
Ten miles above the earth he rose
In his astounding vehicle.

What is the colour of outer space
Above the mountain snows?
Purple and violet, sombre, deep—
But look, down down he goes;

He will not sleep in the stars tonight
Or camp on Augsberg's peaks;
Seventeen hundred fathoms down
Another world he seeks,

And hardly pausing to change his craft
Or see that it is safe
Down to the Ponza Deep he dives
In his strange bathyscaphe.

The yellow light dies out in green,
The green dies out in purple
And all in utter blackness now
Swim round him the sea's people,

The shadowy fish with bulging eyes
The flying phosphorescence,
The mighty shapes that loom in the shades
That never have known man's presence.

But now they know for here he comes
As radiant and orbicular
The bathyscaphe sinks with Piccard inside
Proud, calm and perpendicular.

Oh like a bubble of living sunlight
Down to the bottom they plunge
Where the specks of jelly drift in the murk
And silently breathes the sponge.

From the top of the sky to the bottom of the sea—
How much I wish I were able
To set Professor Piccard now
In his appropriate fable:

How like some mythological hero
Down in that shuddering dark
He wrestled for life with an octopus
Or fought with a giant shark;

How some great lumbering whale or ray
Mistaking him for Jonah
Loomed from the shadowy fog and swallowed
The bathyscaphe and its owner;

Or how like some new Orpheus
Wandering through dim Hades
He saw the queen of the mermaids there
Surrounded by all her ladies

And up and up she followed him,
Divinely fishy and fair,
Out from the dark and the purple gloom
To the breaking wave and the air,

Until at last as the bathyscaphe
Rose bubbling out of the water
The professor yearned for his gleaming prize
And so looked back and lost her.

Or how when he rose up and flew
High to the sun like Icarus
Down from that light he fell, he fell
Through space as black as licorice.

Or like some modern saint, more happily,
Soaring in his uprightness
He felt in his strange globular car
A lift, a sudden lightness,

And saw bright angels wafting him,
Their feathers soft as pullets,
Impervious to cosmic rays
And meteorites like bullets,

To his celestial home. Alas,
He did not see one feather
But studied in the stratosphere
The cosmic rays and the weather;

And when he dived to the floor of the sea
All eager though he stood,
The bathyscaphe half-buried itself
And he saw nothing but mud.

Yet when I think how from that deep
Where life first moved and flickered
His craft rose up like some great egg
And hatched Professor Piccard,

When I reflect how his brave stance
Of perpendicularity
In posture and in motion both
Is man's whole singularity,

Who rose from that same depth and stood
And climbs on to infinity,
He seems more legendary now
Than any old divinity;

And up towards the stars of heaven
Or down to look at zero
I leave Professor Piccard now,
Our emblem and our hero.

THE SILKWORMS

All their lives in a box! What generations,
What centuries of masters, not meaning to be cruel
But needing their labour, taught these creatures such patience
That now though sunlight strikes on the eye's dark jewel
Or moonlight breathes on the wing they do not stir
But like the ghosts of moths crouch silent there.

146

Look it's a child's toy! There is no lid even,
They can climb, they can fly, and the whole world's their tree;
But hush, they say in themselves, we are in prison.
There is no word to tell them that they are free,
And they are not; ancestral voices bind them
In dream too deep for wind or word to find them.

Even in the young, each like a little dragon
Ramping and green upon his mulberry leaf,
So full of life, it seems, the voice has spoken:
They hide where there is food, where they are safe,
And the voice whispers, "Spin the cocoon,
Sleep, sleep, you shall be wrapped in me soon."

Now is their hour, when they wake from that long swoon;
Their pale curved wings are marked in a pattern of leaves,
Shadowy for trees, white for the dance of the moon;
And when on summer nights the buddleia gives
Its nectar like lilac wine for insects mating
They drink its fragrance and shiver, impatient with waiting,

They stir, they think they will go. Then they remember
It was forbidden, forbidden, ever to go out;
The Hands are on guard outside like claps of thunder,
The ancestral voice says Don't, and they do not.
Still the night calls them to unimaginable bliss
But there is terror around them, the vast, the abyss,

And here is the tribe that they know, in their known place,
They are gentle and kind together, they are safe for ever,
And all shall be answered at last when they embrace.
White moth moves closer to moth, lover to lover.
There is that pang of joy on the edge of dying—
Their soft wings whirr, they dream that they are flying.

NESTING TIME

Oh never in this hard world was such an absurd
Charming utterly disarming little bird,
The mossy green, the sunlit honey-eater
That darts from scribbly-gum to banksia tree
And lights upon the head of my small daughter.

It must decide, for men and birds alike,
As pick-pick-pick it goes with its sharp beak,
If so much trust is possible in Nature;
And back it darts to that safe banksia tree
Then swoops on my own head, the brave wild creature.

It thinks it must have hair to line its nest
And hair will have, and it will chance the rest;
And up and down my neck and then my daughter's
Those prickly black feet run, that tugging beak,
And loud like wind it whirrs its green wing-feathers.

Then take your choice from me or those fair tresses
You darting bird too shy for our caresses;
There's just this gap in Nature and in man
Where birds may perch on heads and pull out hair
And if you want to chance it, well, you can.

SARCOCHILUS FITZGERALDI

Here's a word for you, Robert D. FitzGerald:
I met your grandfather living under a stone,
Changed to a small green orchid; where the knobbled
Dripping red cliff-face towered and the creek fell down
Through bracken and wattle, rock-fall and wilderness
To the chasm where the lyrebird sang; yes, there he stood,
Safe on the very brink of bushfire and flood,
Sarcochilus fitzgeraldi, no less!

148

Who would have thought a man could shrink so small?
Deputy Surveyor once of New South Wales,
Now all he surveys on the edge of that wild rock-fall,
In his sandstone crevice where even the sunlight pales,
Is a trickle of the creek, one yard of shadowy sand
Under his golden roof; small space enough
For the tall man striding the mountains, urgent with love
For all those rocky miles could put in his hand.

Yet what's the size of the spirit, and what's its shape?
Here in the spring, forever eager and young
While still that lyrebird breaks the eternal sleep
Of the depths below with sweet and radiant song,
Note upon note in one long crystal shower,
And faint tongue-orchids wake in their cover of moss,
He shall be still what most he loved and was:
Deep under rock, sarcochilus in flower.

Wherefore these words, FitzGerald. It was high time,
After these twenty years, to write acknowledging
Your company in our craft and struggle of rhyme
Where we, like the strider of mountains, have gone foraging
By cliff and creek for the flower among the stones,
That shower of delight the lyrebird sings so readily;
So now I salute you both, all his green family,
In this small tuft of leaves, your grandfather once.

It is like his own hand rising through the rock
With cool green fingers flourishing there most secretly
To startle the traveller with a dead man's look
And move in his mind with images of eternity.
And may you, too, and so may I be seen,
In a hundred years when we have fallen in our turn
Down the abyss where the lyrebird sings in the fern,
Green as sarcochilus, orchid of the ravine.

FIRETAIL FINCHES

Such flashing joy of flower and feather
Over the rock and wild creek-water,
Such ragged scrub and such confusion
Of perching green and flying crimson
Where bottlebrushes tweak themselves
Clean off the twigs with scarlet tails
And finches dart and take their places
Like crimson blossoms on the bushes
And sing in sunlight—it is clear
This joy in Nature does not care
Whether it breaks in bottlebrush clump
Or small bird's beak or small bird's rump
But out through feather and leaf it slips
To deck them all with crimson tips.

LYREBIRD

And cannot always—pick pick pick—be fluting
And floating—pick—down there with fall and fern
Like fern and fall myself; have these exciting
Bugs to find in moss, dead leaves to turn,
So busy here—pick pick—with pick and fluster
Scratching for food like any old red rooster.

Say pheasant then. But plain, but drab, red-brown,
Colour of weathered sandstone, dry withering leaves,
Old applegum bark—pick pick—cooked by the sun;
And am but leaves, am rock from the standstone shelves
Somehow running about; if bird you heard,
Then very happy—pick—just being a bird.

There is a stillness, true, when you look up,
There is a spray of light that falls through trees,
There is a clear cool voice of mountain thrush;
How emerald gleams the moss! And say that these,
Old kookaburra turned to crystal water,
Each smallest trill of robin, wren, tree-creeper,

Currawong's cry, sweet honey-eater's call,
So pierce me through like shafts of moonlight waking
My silent dells that I must be them all
And sing them out with every feather shaking
Like mist down there till all the rock-walls ring;
Why, yes—pick pick—it is a pretty thing. . . .

So round the emerald cliff and out of sight
And filled the gully twice with silver light.

WINDY NIGHT

You foolish wind,
You rush and you blow
All the dark night
Outside my window.

Love is more wise,
It falls to rest
When the wild breath subsides
After the tempest.

Blow, then, you restless,
Make softer and deep
The hollow of quiet
Where my love lies asleep.

THE PICTURES

So that is how my pictures spend their time
(That have all time to spend) when no one's looking
And only moonlight comes to visit them
Or silent midnight up the dark stairs creaking:
Needing no commendation, fearing no fall,
Quietly living their own lives on the wall.

There's Percy Lindsay's ploughman he set up high
Among white glittering cloud and the blue of noon;
He painted his own happiness into the sky
And all through midnight keeps this time of his own;
There like a dark-green wall stands Blamire Young;
He found a sheep-track up to the bird's song.

There silently crashing down on cliff and boulder
Glimmers Lance Solomon's wave in its white swirl;
There Margaret Coen's magnolias curve and smoulder
Like coals of moonlight, like a naked girl;
There half in the light, still half in the shadows' mesh,
The wistfulness of spirit caught in flesh,

Shines the dark grace of Norman Lindsay's Rita,
Breathing unearthly stillness. How strange it seems
I should have walked with, talked with, known these people
On whose clear art the light so moves and gleams;
And one entrusted me for my safe-keeping,
My wife now in the next room quietly sleeping.

These were the people high and far and lonely;
Laughed, loved and lived indeed; and yet were bidden
Walk outside life, care nothing, so that only
They might distil from the visible world its hidden
Order and grace and clarity. As they have done
Here in their pictures cool as the light of the moon.

Woman and flower and wave, gleaming and shadowy,
Seen for the first time in their full reality
They burn now in the moonlight's soft intensity
Like ghosts on the wall: that light is from eternity.
It moves from sky to petal, from foam to face
And fills my night with their immortal grace.

THE DRYAD

There is a dryad in the lemon
But which, but which is she
In all those shapes so like a woman
That nestle in the tree?

If I could tell what tender pair
Of pointed breasts are hers
Among so many clustering there
Where soft the green leaf stirs,

If I could see what deep recess
Of shadow hides her hair
And all that dappled nakedness,
I'd stretch my hand to her;

But love and light and thorny branch
And nymph and lemon-tree
They mingle so I can but watch,
But watch and let her be.

KOOKABURRAS

I see we have undervalued the kookaburras;
They think they are waking the world, and I think so, too.
They gobble the night in their throats like purple berries,
They plunge their beaks in the tide of darkness and dew
And fish up long rays of light; no wonder they howl
In such a triumph of trumpets, leaves fall from the trees,
Small birds fly backwards, snakes disappear in a hole.
And all day long they will rule the bush as they please.

Perched on high branches, cocking sharp eyes for the snake,
From treetop to treetop they watch the sun and follow it;
Far in the west they take it in that great beak
And bang it against a bluegum branch and swallow it;
Then nothing is left in the world but the kookaburras
Like waterfalls exulting down the gullies.

GOLDFISH

Sunlight-red and river-green,
In and out and round and round
From sunken stone to floating leaf
My goldfish rove the lily-pond.

They have no thought except to eat
(The red one chews the water-weed)
Or dart in sudden freaks of play
Clean through the shoal at topmost speed.

They nibble at the feet of wasps,
They prowl for algae in the lilies
Or standing on their heads deep down
Display a flash of silver bellies.

They know my hand that drops them food
Is no black wing of hurt and trouble;
And, scorning crane or kookaburra,
Up they come and how they gobble!

Then one in frolic swirls his tail,
Pretending fish must not be seen,
And off they dart and fill my pool
With sunlight-red and river-green.

WATERLILY

Look, look, there is an angel in the fishpond,
It wakes its yellow wings above the water;
Or say the naked moon came down to bathe here
And dipped her toe in weeds and so we caught her;
Or say the sun fell in and sprang up yellow,
Or say that mud's in flower today—no matter:
All images and fancies coalesce and cancel
In mystery at last; it is an angel,
And moves its yellow wings above the water.

LEOPARD SKIN

Seven pairs of leopard-skin underpants
Flying on the rotary clothes-line! Oh, look, look, virgins,
How with the shirts and pyjamas they whirl and dance.
And think no more, trembling in your own emergence
Like butterflies into the light, that tall soft boy
Who nightly over his radio crooned and capered
Alone in his room in weird adolescent joy
Is mother's boy, softy: has he not slain a leopard?

But more than that: does he not wear its skin,
Secretly, daily, superbly? Oh, girls, adore him,
For dreaming on velvet feet to slay and to sin
He prowls the suburb, the wild things flee before him,
He miaous at the leopardesses, and they stop:
He *is* a leopard—he bought himself in a shop.

FENCE

Fence must be looked at; fence is too much neglected;
Most ancient indeed is fence; but it is not merely
White ants' and weather's ravage must be inspected,
The broken paling where we can see too clearly
The neighbours at their affairs, that larger hole
Where Hogan's terrier ate it, or very nearly;
But fence most quintessential, fence in its soul.

For fence is *defensa*, Latin; fence is old Roman
And heaven knows what wild tribes, rude and unknown,
It sprang from first, when man took shelter with his woman;
Fence is no simple screen where Hogan may prune
His roses decently hidden by paling or lattice
Or sporting together some sunny afternoon
Be noticed with Mrs Hogan at nymphs and satyrs;

But fence is earthwork, *defensa*; connected no doubt
With *fossa*, a moat; straight from the verb to defend;
Therefore ward off, repel, stand guard on the moat;
None climbs this fence but cat or Hogan's friend.
Fence is of spears and brambles; fence is defiance
To sabre-toothed tigers, to all the world in the end,
And there behind it the Hogans stand like lions.

It is not wise to meet the Hogans in quarrel,
They have a lawyer and he will issue writs;
Thieves and trespassers enter at deadly peril,
The brave dog bites the postman where he sits.
Just as they turn the hose against the summer's
Glare on the garden, so in far fiercer jets
Here they unleash the Hogans against all comers.

True it is not very often the need arises
And they are peaceable people behind their barrier;
But something is here that must be saved in a crisis,
They know it well and so does the sharp-toothed terrier.
They bring him bones, he worships them deeply and dankly,
He thinks Mrs Hogan a queen and Hogan a warrior,
Most excellent people, and they agree with him, frankly.

The world, they feel, needs Hogans; they can contribute
To its dull pattern all their rich singularity;
And if, as is true, it pays them no proper tribute,
Hogans from Hogans at least shall not lack charity.
Shielded by fences are they not free to cherish
Each bud, each shoot, each fine particularity
Which in the Hogans burgeons and must not perish?

It is not just that their mighty motor mower
Roars loudest for miles and chops up the insolent grass,
Nor that the Iceland poppies are dancing in flower,
Nor the new car all shiny with chromium and glass,
Nor the fridge and T.V., nor that, the bloom of their totem,
Their freckled children always come first in the class
Or sometimes at least, and never are seen at the bottom;

It is all this and so much more beside
Of Hogans down the ages in their proud carriage
And Hogan young and Mrs Hogan a bride
And napkins washed and babies fumbling their porridge,
Things which no prying stranger can know or feel—
All locked in the strange intimacy of marriage,
Which by all means let decent fences conceal.

So let us to work, good neighbour, this Saturday morning,
Nail up the paling so Hogans are free to be Hogans
And Stewarts be Stewarts and no one shall watch us scorning
And no one break in with bullets and bombs and slogans
Or we will stand guard at the fence and fight as we can.
World is against us, but world has had its warning;
Deep out of time is fence and deep is man.

TERRIGAL

How lucky are the children of Terrigal—
How can they possibly tell
If it is birds in the branches
Or school that is ringing its bell?

Down in that valley of bellbirds
When morning is green and cool,
With that sweet din all around them
How can they find their school?

Straight goes the road through the cuttings
And that is the safest and surest
But how can they find their direction
With hundreds of bells in the forest?

Loud is the bell for the roll-call,
Tall is the teacher and stern,
But try as they will they get lost there
Deep among sunlight and fern.

How lucky are the children of Terrigal
Where all the air is so full
Of the ringing and dinging of bellbirds
They never can get to school.

Nobody shuts them in classrooms
To yearn at the windowpane,
They have walked out of the window
And no one can find them again.

Nobody plagues them with poetry,
Nobody stuns them with sums,
They can count ripples on water
Or add up the she-oaks and gums.

All they have set for their homework
When they come home for their tea
Is, what is the mood of a bellbird
When it says ding in a tree?

People grow up very seriously
Stuffed with dull figures and words:
How lucky are the children of Terrigal,
They're filled with the music of birds.

A COUNTRY SONG

Schute, Bell, Badgery, Lumby,
How's your dad and how'd your mum be?
What's the news, oh, far from here
Under the blue sky burning clear
Where your beautiful business runs
Wild as a dingo, fresh as a brumby?

Lumby, Badgery, Bell, Schute,
Pipe me a song, for I am mute,
Of red earth growing you hides and tallow,
Rivers wandering brown and shallow
And old grey gum-trees never dead
While magpies play them like a flute.

Bell, Lumby, Schute, Badgery,
How's the world in your menagerie?—
Hennessey's stallion and Hogan's bull,
Sheds at Yass crammed full with wool,
Heifers and vealers, rams and lambs,
From Nimmitabel to Wantabadgery.

Badgery, Schute, Lumby, Bell,
How's the world? The world goes well.
The auctioneer, that merry man,
Out in the sleet at Queanbeyan
Swigged his whisky neat from the bottle
And up went prices while buyers fell.

Schute, Bell, Badgery, Lumby,
Town's all stone and stone so dumb be.
Past Wee Jasper I remember
The ewes drew out through the green timber . . .
Oh what's your price for all that country
Wild as a dingo, fresh as a brumby?

THREE WHITE HERONS

Nonsense, they're artificial. It is some farmer
Or farmer's wife has a whim for such commodities
And white by the dam in the she-oaks' dusky murmur
Has set them there for company or for oddities,
Three porcelain herons . . . as some divert themselves
With frogs and toads and toadstools, gnomes and elves,

All sorts of grotesqueness. It is a recognition
Of some need of the earth Nature forgot to fulfil,
Something which ought to be there but certainly isn't,
Or not in these stiff herons—standing so still,
Wry-necked, hump-backed, frozen on one black leg,
You'd think they all hatched out of a china egg—

And so they did, three porcelain birds together.
True, it is easy enough to be wrong about herons—
That beak went snap? Some ruffle of a wind-stirred feather?
The movement of shadows may give some faint appearance . . .
But much too faint to claim it a sign of life.
Let us drive on and ask the farmer's wife.

THE DRY CREEK

I cannot catch this water,
Not even now when it's gone
And dry lies the creek in the paddock
With all its secrets shown,
Shallow and pool and eddy,
Clay, shingle and stone.

Like the brown thirsty sheep
I ponder sand and pebble:
Here's that long-buried stump
The current used to nibble,
Here the blue heron fished,
Here frogs cried out like a bubble.

Not the most crystal water
Was ever as this so clear:
All I can not see now
Is my own face when I peer,
Looking for something gone
Yet still mysteriously here.

How like a woman she lies,
Who once was a shy wild girl
Sparkling through the green grasses
With all her skirt in a whirl!—
Grown dry and brown and older,
Haunted by water still,

Children and lovers all gone,
Youth vanished past recall,
Bare to the sun she abandons
Her body's curve and fall
In the last inviolable secret
Of having no secrets at all.

THE MAN FROM ADAMINABY

Hard to say where he came from—
Maybe the Great Divide
Where the sun like a golden raindrop
Rolls down Kiandra side,

Or down from Kelly's high plains
With his pick-axe over his shoulder
Or out of a hollow snowgum
Or out of a granite boulder—

Or maybe he came from Bugtown
That's far enough out and further
Though there isn't any town at Bugtown
And there aren't any bugs there either.

Anyway on his white horse
He rode down out of the hills,
His pick-axe over his shoulder,
His two black dogs at his heels.

—"A long way back to Kiandra,
Miles further than you'd think,
Where the mullock-heaps glint on the hillside
And the white snow-daisies wink;

A long way back to Kiandra
Over the blue sky's brink
But here's old Adaminaby
Where a man can get a drink.

Cool are the bar and the beer there,
And my old mates gathered round" . . .
—"You'll wait a long time for a drink, mate,
The blooming pub's been drowned."

—"Seen a high tide myself there,
The beer right up to our necks". . .
—"She's sunk like a ship, we tell you,
With all the rest of the wrecks.

Where have you been these years
With your mare and your dogs and your pick?
The whole town's under the water,
Pisé and stone and brick.

While you were sinking your shaft, mate,
Or shearing, was it, or droving,
They shut the old pub right down, mate,
They brought in early-closing.

The publican, none too soon,
Has finally lost his licence;
Chimney and shadowy door there
Drink to each other in silence.

Only the shag like a copper
Dives down to the window to peer;
Yabbies crawl over the counter,
Mud-eyes are into the beer.

At the bar door the bunyip
Lies down and scratches his fleas:
And a great wave of the Snowy
Says 'Time, gentlemen, please.'

There's drink enough still of a kind, mate,
If your taste runs far as water,
It's over the café, too, mate,
It's over the tallest poplar.

But the beer she's off for ever
And so is Adaminaby,
It's all under water making
Hydroelectricity."

—"Hydroelectricity
Don't make no sense to me
And there's the whole town still standing
So far as I can see.

It runs right down to the farms there
Under the shining air
And pink the apple trees bloom there,
Like a white cloud the pear.

She's the old town as ever
And all my mates will remember me
When I go down as always
To drink in Adaminaby."

—"She's drowned, she's gone, she's flooded!"
—"Ah, tell the marines," he cried,
And called his black dogs to him
And spurred the white mare's side,

And rode on down the hillside
As he had done for years
And straight out under the water
And drank there with his peers.

YARRANGOBILLY

How can a little bird with a brain like a feather
Provide against so many dire emergencies?
For snake and fox, yes, butcherbird and weather,
Both fire and flood, but hardly these great savages
Who stumbling down the limestone gorge discover
Those four pink eggs that match the teatree blossom,
That cup of lichen trembling over the river,
Looped on the twig there like a wisp of flotsam.

But chirp in peace you small green honeyeater
Who hung your nest so cunningly over the water;
We'll do no more than brood with you upon it
Till we have hatched those eggs out in a sonnet
That catches in its music, soft or shrilly,
Something of bird-song, something of Yarrangobilly.

BIRD AND MAN

While river browns and beats its stones
And sally-gum shines wet and bronze

Rain pours over the mountain top
And bird looks down and man looks up.

Man's that tall one, wades the water,
Waves a rod and flicks a feather,

A most mysterious thing to do
In the eye of a big grey cockatoo.

Bird is gang-gang, well he knows
His whole head's feathered like a rose;

If to bob it isn't enough
He can bite a twig clean off.

Watch and glow or climb and dance,
Never doubt my admiring glance,

But I am glad, old cockatoo
That I can also interest you,

Man and gang-gang, so we share
A moment's equal pleasure here;

And wish that I had more to offer
Than what a man is by a river

Before you fly so soon again
Like a wild rose into the rain.

A FLOCK OF GANG-GANGS

So many gang-gangs dark as banksia-cones
As red as red grevilleas I see now
In that white tree above the water and stones
There seem to be two birds on every bough.

And more and more come in and as they fly
And settle on the branches clear or hidden
In light and leaves they cry their creaking cry
As though the tree were cracking with the burden.

There is the sound of granite in their voices,
Of rocks in ice, high up and harsh and wintry,
And yet in their soft plumes summer rejoices
In flame and charcoal, so they fit the country.

Some sleep like flowers big and soft and dark,
Some lift their crests up in a crimson ruffle
And light the leaves of that old candlebark
Or make it dance as they bob heads and shuffle;

Some sharpen their great beaks on hard dead wood
And nip the twigs off in a leafy rain,
Some spread their wings and flare in fighting mood
That's all pretence, then fall to sleep again;

Some preen each other, some to show their skill
Hang upside down like bats from the high branches
While drowsy lovers nibble bill to bill
With horny kisses and with sidelong glances.

Two four six eight, yes twenty-two I count
Keeping this happy company with each other,
And watch one sly young opportunist mount
His startled mate and both fall off together.

Sleeping or dancing, gossiping or loving
In that white tree with sun and blue sky over,
All of one mind, it's certain they are having
A great day to remember by the river,

So when one soft grey feather flutters down
I pick it up before cold time can take it
Or lose it where the fallen leaves lie brown
And put it, with this poem, in my pocket.

RATA

"Curse these birds," said Rata, "and curse their cousins,
Sandfly, stonefly, dragonfly and gnat,
For there's no doubt that swarming in their thousands

It's they who've knocked my dearest work down flat,
Or rather stood it up—in these confusions
Of whirring wings and feathers, I don't know what—

But there, look there, with humming and with trilling,
Some tugging at the crown, some carting chips,
No bird not busy, no beetle that's unwilling,

The veriest midge with sawdust on his lips,
The hairy kiwi pushing, pigeons pulling,
They launch my tree in air as on the slips,

As from the slips where it should now be sailing!
I thought to make myself a small canoe
Or large as it might be, good luck prevailing;

It was a simple thing that I could do,
No harm to anyone, no fear of failing,
And take the seas with it where waves are blue

For we have crouched in forests far too long.
Oh, I'd have seats in it for forty rowers,
Who'd sail with me, my kinsmen tall and strong,

And cut its lines as graceful as the kowhai's
And carve a god on it with lolling tongue
To lick the waves and scare their salty powers—

So came each day, oh, glad at daybreak came
Through fern and vine and singing enemies
(I thought were happy birds), and by the stream

Chopped down that mightiest tree among the trees
And worked on it; and monstrous, like a dream,
Saw it next morning towering in the breeze

Rebuilt by birds and insects! There it stands,
The tree, the tree, the tree that I cut down,
My dear canoe, the work of my own hands,

That I had shaped and hollowed, all undone,
Growing untouched beside the pebbly sands.
Must I, for birds, do all my work again?"

And bursting from the forest where he'd hidden,
He caught the nearest fantail by the tail.
—"Master, we do but do as we are bidden;

Canoes are good, and good it is to sail
On far blue seas, but we are Tane's children
And Tane says no tree of his must fall.

You chop it down: the god says, 'Put together!' "
—"The sea has also gods, all crisp with foam,
They call me out to meet the wild blue weather."

—"Then say," the fantail said, "you cannot come."
Rata pulled out that little bird's tail-feather
And scratched his head with it, and so went home.

There is a sweet forgivingness in things,
Say what you will, that does at last relent
When it has stunned us with its buffetings,

For lo, next morning when poor Rata went
Once more to strive with all those beaks and wings
That for so long had mocked his best intent,

There his canoe lay shining in the thicket!
Now whether Tane in his vast green mind
Thought prudent to placate his friend the seagod

Whose waves could sweep the island where he reigned,
Or maybe just got tired of being wicked
Or even thought one moment to be kind,

Having so many trees that he could spare
(There is no questioning a wood-god's morals),
Certain it is the craft lay shining there

And whirling round his head with chirps and carols
And calls and whistles bright as morning air,
The birds begged Rata to forget their quarrels,

For they had toiled to make it all night long;
And there were seats in it for forty rowers
To sail with him, his kinsmen tall and strong,

And sweetly slept its lines among the flowers,
And they had carved a god with crimson tongue
To ride its prow and scare the salty powers—

It shone there like an answer to his prayer.
"Then bless the birds and all their small relations,"
Cried Rata plucking beetles from his hair;

And took the stream and sailed for the bright oceans
And waved good-bye to all his pain and care,
Thanking the gods, although with reservations.

THE GARDEN OF SHIPS

Even so deep in the jungle they were not safe.
The stars still glittered round them like barbed wire
But more than that, fantastic below the cliff
A lantern filled a tree with orange fire
Like a great tropical flower, one window's gleam
With a round yellow eye stared up at them.

If it was another village of the dog-faced people
As seemed most likely, no one ran out to bark;
And the tree seemed bare and tapering, more like a steeple
Where the light like a golden bell rocked in the dark.
Was it the mast of a ship?—impossibly lost
Here in the forest, mile upon mile from the coast?

They could climb down and creep on it through the jungle
For lights meant men, and men meant water and food
And they were thirsty enough, and they were hungry;
But when had the lights of men ever brought them good?
Not in these evil islands, not in these times;
But years ago, it seemed, in the country of dreams.

All night long they talked about it in whispers.
They would have liked to sleep, for they had come far
By burning and naked seas, by sliding rivers,
By islands smouldering still with the smoke of war
Or shrouded in steam, to reach this ridge at last;
But how could they sleep with that strange light on the mast?

And sometimes water glimmered, sometimes it seemed
That ranging away from the lantern, tree by tree
Or mast by mast, whole fleets of vessels gleamed
Faint in the starshine where no ships could be.
And in the morning they were ships indeed!
It was amazing, Marco Polo said,

Speaking of his own travels to that island,
How such a current surged there through the ocean
It seized upon wandering ships and dragged them inland;
And leaping against the hills in white explosion
Tore by their roots the tall trees out of the jungle;
And up the long gulf, in one vast helpless tangle,

Swept them along, tall ships and trees together,
And drove more timber in and piled it up
So they lay locked at the end of the gulf for ever
While many a merchant mourned his missing ship.
But what was more amazing, though for that matter
Likely enough to happen with trees and water,

Was how while the ships lay still as they did now
High-decked, tall-masted, flotsam from all the seas,
Junks from old China, sampan, Arabian dhow,
Galleon and barque, Dutch, English, Portuguese,
Their anchors green with moss, their sails all furled,
Never again to ride the waves of the world,

That wall of trees, as silt filled up the shallows,
Took root again and stood up tall and green
And taller grew and flung their leafy shadows
From ship to ship with flowering vines between,
Hanging the masts with such enchanting burden
It seemed the fleet was anchored in a garden.

And there were gardeners too—that was the thing,
Piercingly strange, that moved the watchers most;
Far down, unseen, they heard a woman sing,
She might have been a bird there, or a ghost;
But windows opened, plumes of smoke rose up,
Brown men in sarongs walked about each ship

And all the jungle rang with children's laughter;
And they saw too, not least of many solaces,
Where bridges joined the ships across the water,
Bare-breasted girls who walked among the trellises
Or white and golden, fair as waterlilies,
Plunged in the pools and swam with gleaming bodies.

So, ragged and bony, wild-eyed with war and fever,
They came down out of the jungle to the clearing
And truly they thought they could lie down there for ever,
Feasting on fruit, drinking the palm-wine, hearing
The laughter and the music, the lap of the tide
Stealing so far from the sea to the ship's side,

And those soft voices telling the old stories
Of how they had lived on the ships for generations,
And if the dog-faced people on their forays
Chanced on their haven, people of all the nations
Living in peace together untouched by the world,
They lifted up their dog-faced heads and howled

And fled, thinking them spirits. So too, long after
When the war and all their journeying turned to a dream,
Like a wild vision they had seen in their fever,
Even to these two wanderers did they seem;
For calling them always with its clear compulsion
Somewhere over the mountains, across the ocean,

With its broad golden fields, its urgent cities,
Its ports where ships still sailed on whatever venture,
Their homeland lay; and though like waterlilies
The fair girls swam and the birds sang in rapture
And the old ships dreamed in the jungle; even so,
Now they were strong they could reach it, and they must go.

172

RUTHERFORD

Mostly too busy to think—too busy thinking.
But thinking was doing; there was such satisfaction
Watching those tiny comets darting and winking
It really left no time for speculation.
Thought would go outwards, expansion; his was a shrinking,
How to get mind and hand so small, that was the problem,
That in one final thrust of concentration
They would be able to move inside an atom.

It was the most fascinating thing in the world
And out of it too, like watching some new star:
To go in there and watch the atom unfold
Its innermost secrets, right to the very core
Where star within star the racing electrons whirled
Circling that radiant centre, the white-hot nucleus,
—Held in your hands, almost, huge as you were,
Pierced by your thought like a neutron. It was miraculous

How out of steel and glass, coiled wire and lead,
The common stuff of the earth (what else could you use?),
Mere human powers could have conceived and made
These infinitely delicate instruments to pierce
Clean through matter to its end. But that was his trade;
He had it if from anyone from his father
And sometimes it seemed, alone in the universe
In the laboratory at night, they worked together,

That craftsman's hands still moving inside his own.
It was a haunted place, this tower of knowledge,
Calm with old books but wild with thoughts unknown,
All dark except for lamps like lights of courage
Where lonely scholars sought for truth in stone.
It shut the whole world out from a man and his work;
But while the white stars glittered above the college
A wheel moved somewhere far away in the dark—

And huge it was, and turned with a soft roar
Of air and water, and battered the dark and scattered
Dewdrops like stars and seemed itself the core
Of that clear atom of night whose peace it shattered
Under the mountain towering there once more!
It seemed the Rutherfords' fate to start things moving.
Yet how the white snow sparkled, the stream glittered,
How tranquilly when his mind moved into morning

That waterwheel of his father's lifted up
Water and sunlight in its wooden hands
Where the weed grew like hair, then let them drop
Back to the stream that sang on over the sands.
Once it had turned that swamp of flax to rope
Useful to man, the river was free to be river
And on its own wheel of boulders wove its strands
Of silver light through green Taranaki for ever—

Such thousands of miles from this great shadowy room
Where only minutely exploding, the alpha particles
Flashed on the screen like sun-motes. But when he had time,
When he was quiet like this, alone among miracles,
Sometimes indeed his mind went wandering home
And, following his father's, his life seemed queer and fated.
For while, even now, dripping its light like icicles
Under the mountain, that wheel still turned as he waited,

And farmers' drays ran jolting through frost and mud
And far by emerald river and ferny hill
In long-lost Nelson wheels that his father had made,
And good wheels too, were serving the people still
—They carried the milk; they ground the flour for bread—
He too was making a wheel; but not for the water,
Not for the road or the mill, but such a wheel
He knew would carry man and all his future.

It was as if in one swift generation
He had bridged the years from the first man to the last,
Run the whole course of human civilization
Since some half-naked craftsman far in the past
First shaped a wheel and set the thing in motion;
All moved on the wheel, and the force that drove the wheel,
And here in this spinning atom he had unloosed
Such motion and force as made the senses reel—

Or would, if you could not control them, but he could!
Dance then, you little atomies! He would untether,
Two jumps ahead of anyone else in the world,
The force that held the universe together
To take man on his journey, go where he would.
And truly, mastering these forces, he would go far,
Exploring into the dark blind mass of matter
Or up to the moon and on from star to star,

Where at last ended perhaps, or did not end,
The trend of all wheels, the highroad of human destiny.
There was a speculation! But when he scanned
One moment over the quadrangle glittering silently
That splendour whose faintest touch would scorch his hand,
Planet and comet and star, cluster and nebulae—
What was he doing with his finger in that immensity?
Wheel beyond wheel and world beyond world to infinity,

The universe turned and moved above him so vast,
Full of black space, the huge wheel slowly spinning,
He knew he stood with his specks of radiant dust
Not at the end of things but at the beginning.
Men would go striding on because they must
But what was he, the famous Lord Rutherford,
While there were still such vastitudes for winning,
But that old savage with his wheel? Good Lord, good Lord,

So much they would surpass him, those who came after,
What was he now but that small lump of a boy
Who made his own miniature wheel to splash in the water
Such ages ago; working all day in the joy
Of pure and bubbling creation, copying his father:
Just so it was small and would work, just so it sparkled.
And yet the truth was, this was a dangerous toy:
The lightning swam where those electrons circled.

Look at it this way, that way, face the thing squarely.
Could some fool in a laboratory, he'd asked his assistants,
Blow up the world with this? You could pay dearly
For probing too deeply into that dark resistance
Where light lay coiled in stone. He had seen clearly
In flashes of the mind each atom exploding the next
To the end of the world, and the light came out of the distance
Like a wave upon him, towering. . . . They were perplexed,

Whether he was joking or not. Well, he was joking.
There was no need to cower, and what was more,
Though sometimes he touched these things with his hands shaking,
He did not propose to; he'd carry the load he bore,
Which was no light one, till his broad shoulders were aching.
But need not, except as precaution, think the unthinkable:
There was no chain-reaction could go so far;
The force must die out; the good old world was unsinkable.

So let his atoms be used to do man good
And nothing but good—pierce to the cancer cell
As the Curies were doing, bring him more health, more food,
Drive the turbine, the dynamo, turn the wheel,
Blow a mountain up if it got in his road.
Let him be master of air and earth and ocean,
The whole wide world and the stars if he liked as well.
He had not given his lifetime's skill and devotion

To bring man harm. And yet this thing was force;
And when could you give poor man and his five wits.
Any new force but he would use it in his wars
And blow himself if not the whole world to bits?
Take off his trappings and, naked, hungry and fierce,
All over the earth, in jungle or civilized city,
Men were but savages yet; God help the poor brutes,
For this new power, appalling to love and pity,

Was force that no savage yet had dreamed of wielding.
Dare he release it? Alone in this still room
With those uncanny electrons whirling and shielding
The inviolable core, he felt he was living in a dream
And he saw towers falling and skyscrapers melting—
Fantastic, inconceivable; yet must be conceived.
Then you could turn away, pack up and go home,
Dismantling the apparatus. And he half believed

This moment that he could do it; get hold of a farm
Snug under snowy Egmont, beside the river,
And there where the frost melted and morning was warm
Stroll down to look at the pigs; there was much in favour
Of pigs, taken as pigs, life's earthiest form;
And in those paddocks there, starry with daisies,
Golden with dandelions, purple with clover,
(How rich was the land!) he'd have his herd of Jerseys,

And up in the dawn to milk them, hitch up the cart,
Off to the factory to yarn with others of his type
(Looked like a farmer, always a farmer at heart,
Corpulent, bushy-moustached, smoking his pipe)
Then feed the skim-dick to the pigs—it was a part
He had played in dreams, planted on that green shelf
With the cows and the oats and the turnips till he grew ripe
And simple and stolid as the good black earth itself . . .

Too stolid, perhaps. Well, you could hire labour,
A sharefarmer, say, and still find plenty worth doing:
Get on the County Council, do good to your neighbour,
Fix up the roads and bridges. And once you got going,
Why not keep on? Be Pungarehu's member
For Parliament, eh? Minister for Agriculture,
Prime Minister then, why not? There was no knowing
Where he would get to in that rustic future,

Who now had got to this room. And there already
That powerful body, that restless mind of his,
As soon as he looked forward with his hand steady
Were driving him still. . . . On just such a journey as this
Where he had climbed as high as anybody
And liked it, too, although at times it shook him.
He had enjoyed so much the work, the success,
Discoveries sparkling like jewels wherever it took him.

"I'll dig no more potatoes!" so he had vowed
That day the telegram from Cambridge came,
And dug no more indeed, nor milked nor ploughed
Except in the great seas of thought and fame;
And where the surf broke high and white and loud
In wonder watched as island after island
Rose in his mind's eye with their dazzling gleam.
So he stood now, Earl Rutherford of Nelson,

The great sea-farer of science. But the room was silent.
Space, so it seemed, looked in upon him like eyes
And it seemed possible in that shattering moment
That just to be a schoolboy winning a prize
He had ended or nearly ended man's life on this planet.
Then no and no and no, he could only assert,
That was not true! Impossible to disguise
That what he had found could do mankind grave hurt,

178

None graver; true, too, he could never go back
And share the old simplicities with his father.
Let them live on! But he had grown to like
This life of power where scientists met together
And felt they were priests and rulers. He liked to talk
With his great peers that language wrapped in mystery—
But he'd be plain if he could. No, it was rather
He liked the thought that what he touched was history,

As in truth it was; he'd have his personal pride.
A man alive must show what he could do.
But that was irrelevant, nothing; something outside
That final, inner truth so well he knew,
Always with that chill in the blood, when hands that had died,
Or hands not human at all, beyond his seeking,
Hands not his own, like a mist, came creeping through
His own at their work and made what he was making.

He was so clumsy and blind, beyond all patience:
But out of the dark, from nowhere, flashed the conception
Like force in the atom and filled him with its radiance;
And steadily, patiently, always in the right direction
Despite his stumblings it moved in him in silence
Until at last what it wanted to do was done.
All things, it seemed, moved through time to perfection,
Through earth and wood and flesh, through the mind of man.

But whether it was some quite unknowable powers
Dark and divine, or simply the spirit of the race
That moved in him and grew these hot small flowers
That bloomed behind lead for safety, when could you trace
Though you sat here watching and watching all the dark hours
Such an imponderable, such an unprovable process?
It was the solid facts he had to face.
Yes, but they gave the same clear answer of progress:

And it was not merely the hand upon the wheel
That led to this, but the whole drive of the mind
Since first that restless radiance tore at its veil,
Rock, flesh and sky, to seek what lay behind.
And what did lie, as the Greeks guessed so well,
Was the whirling atoms; and what was the implication
Of that, God alone knew; but here, combined,
Thought and the hand had lit our civilization

With what it had dreamed of: not just his own ambition
But all mankind's, Lord knows what power beside,
Came here to some great moment of fruition
And into the future cast its glittering seed.
So now in God's name, thinking of nuclear fission
And looking out of the window into the dark
Where lay the whole teeming world that man had made,
London, Paris, Berlin, Moscow, New York,

How stop mankind destroying it? Easy to say
That only science could turn this force to destruction
And science must not; but fierily though it lay
On each man's conscience, there was such soft seduction
In science itself, and power and place and pay,
You could do evil or fall into taking a bribe
Almost without your knowing; and, clear of corruption,
Still you could make your conscience that of the tribe

And do its bidding without one trace of guilt
But rather, as he knew well, with a clear ardour.
And when the old passions were roused and blood was spilt
And the enemy hordes came swarming over the border
Like Gaul and the Hun again, like Scythian or Celt,
Civilized men in Europe killing and ravaging,
What else could man do but stand against the marauder?
That was the thing that must change, this pattern of savaging.

It was an old habit men had got into
Far back in the forest, grasping more food for the clan,
And served its purpose in quickening mind and sinew;
But now since it threatened the whole existence of man
We must not, could not, dare not let it continue.
And there was the crux, perhaps, in that word "dare";
For never had there been such a weapon since time began
And men who would stop at nothing might stop at fear.

But this was the great high tide of power and thought
And not all men were savages—that was the certainty
That buoyed him up against these winds of doubt:
Think of such colleagues now as Hahn in Germany—
Good God, could he cross the Channel and cut his throat?
Men had outgrown such horror. He put his trust,
Despite the whole long course of human barbarity,
In what must supplant it, the rule of the strong and the just.

There would be place enough still for all the old chivalry
While half the world was savage; but now began,
Now must begin, a clear new turn in history,
And there in his atoms, cramped in so small a span,
It glittered before him and rayed away out to infinity.
How perilous and dark, how enigmatic a course
It seemed to set whirling there for the race of man
Now bound to the inmost force of the universe—

And yet as he looked at the sky so dark with warning
Vast over earth and its towers, the night heaved over
Close and familiar as a waterwheel turning
And shed its stars like drops of crystal water
And radiant over the world lay the clear morning.
Men moved in darkness truly, but also in the sun
And on that huge bright wheel that turned for ever
He left his thought, for there was work to be done.

LATER POEMS

THE FLOWERING PLACE

Hedge and fence and old stone wall
Shut the island in securely,
Elm and oak-tree grow so tall
There's no chance to see too clearly;
Yet all flowers grow between
Savage snow and jungle green.

Kingdon Ward on Karpo Razi
Gathering rhododendron seed
Climbed because the slope was easy
High, far higher than he need
And on the rock-ledge stopped appalled
To see the naked edge of the world.

Miles to the green haze below
Fell the precipice from his feet;
Bleak with ice and wild with snow
Peak and crag leapt up to meet
Reeling in the wind's cold shock
Barren space with barren rock.

From that ledge so bare so crazy,
Down through shale and tussock came
To eyebright, primula, silver daisy,
First small sparks of living flame;
And midway down the stony screes
Saw again the low hard trees

That he had known in glowing spring
Purple and crimson, mauve and white,
The fragile acres blossoming
Between green gulf and icy height;
And there from each brown flower head
Took the rhododendrons' seed,

And down, came down to that wild stream
Where shaking in its rainbow's shower
Like snow and light distilled in dream
He'd seen the first azalea flower;
And left that last clear light and stood
Where warm as steam and rank as blood

Writhing and thick in one green tangle
Gross with rain and fierce with heat
Cruel nature swarmed in the jungle,
Tree fought tree to reach the light.
Through the glades where silently
The strangling vine crept up the tree,

And out into the shining sun;
Over the long dry burning plain
And ship and sea and, journey done,
Back from Burma and home again
To elm and oak-tree's gentle shade;
And knowing how the world was made

Saw when now like lights of dream
On their far-off mountainside
White azalea lit its gleam,
Rhododendron flared in pride,
All his island flowered between
Savage snow and jungle green.

B FLAT

Sing softly, Muse, the Reverend Henry White
Who floats through time as lightly as a feather
Yet left one solitary gleam of light
Because he was the Selborne naturalist's brother

And told him once how on warm summer eves
When moonlight filled all Fyfield to the brim
And yearning owls were hooting to their loves
On church and barn and oak-tree's leafy limb

He took a common half-a-crown pitch-pipe
Such as the masters used for harpsichords
And through the village trod with silent step
Measuring the notes of those melodious birds

And found that each one sang, or rather hooted,
Precisely in the measure of B flat.
And that is all that history has noted;
We know no more of Henry White than that.

So, softly, Muse, in harmony and conformity
Pipe up for him and all such gentle souls
Thus in the world's enormousness, enormity,
So interested in music and in owls;

For though we cannot claim his crumb of knowledge
Was worth much more than virtually nil
Nor hail him for vast enterprise or courage,
Yet in my mind I see him walking still

With eager ear beneath his clerical hat
Through Fyfield village sleeping dark and blind,
Oh surely as he piped his soft B flat
The most harmless, the most innocent of mankind.

THE PEAHEN

A Meditation on Natural Selection

And pondered much on peahens, a curious study
For manifestly it was this miserable bird
Conversing in doleful whimperings, humble and muddy
Before the jewelled splendours of her lord,
Who nevertheless with exquisite taste had chosen
That fiery pattern in which his pride was frozen.

Both the alternatives were too absurd.
There was no special creation, that was admitted;
No one named God had said, Let there be bird,
Let bird be peacock, lo let peacocks be fitted
With comets behind them. . . . So pleasing and clear a solution
Defied the whole known facts of evolution.

Nor could you reasonably say such coloration,
All gold and blue and never one sober feather,
The noonday breast, the tail's bright constellation,
Grew to protect the peacock from the tiger.
Any old browns or greens would have served to mingle
The bird more satisfactorily with the jungle.

So it was clear that after the strange mutation
When the first scaly lizard grew the first feather
And grew two more, or twenty, the next generation,
Till lizards at last had changed into birds altogether
And shrinking and stretching, changing to brighter or duller,
Peacocks and wrens evolved their form and their colour,

In the tribe of the peafowl it was the females who did it:
Not any timorous cock plunging for cover
Deeper into the jungle dark that hid it
But the fastidious peahen choosing her lover:
Some drab old cock grew one blue feather in his breast
And lo the peahen loved him past all the rest.

Or some chance tail-feather trailed like a reed in the swamp
Or stood erect and danced in the air like a fairy
And all the peahens eyeing its primitive pomp
Thought, That is the tail-feather I was born to marry.
They did not rush, they did not claw and tear him
But being modest females, sat down near him.

What of the other cocks unable to please?
They walked alone and grieved with unearthly howls,
They jumped from high cliffs, they hanged themselves in the trees;
But proudly the chosen bridegroom strutted with his fowls
And begot on them fabulous progeny, more and more splendid,
More royally breasted and crested, more regally ended.

And deep in the jungle humid and dark and sultry,
Selecting, rejecting, mating the finest each time,
Generations of hens, those most poetical poultry,
Watched that each feather fell into place like a rhyme,
Feather by blue breast-feather nestling and tinkling,
Feather by feather the tail's great fountain sprinkling,

Until at some point in time, we cannot say when,
There was an end at last to natural selection:
Far in some glade of the forest beside his hen,
Shining from top to tail in final perfection
The ultimate cock stood blazing like rays of the sun,
And shyly she whimpered, knowing her task was done.

That was the process, and most satisfactory to know it. . . .
But then if we saw some peacock burning in vision
Who yawped his barbaric yawp, himself like a poet,
And stared with his hundred eyes in dark derision
And drummed his wings and shook his great fan of feathers,
That theory seemed nonsensical as all the others.

It could not be sufficient explanation;
And if it were, what of the peahen's mind
We'd proved responsible for his creation?
Instinct or taste in her was so refined
That she who had made him perfect and sought no sequel
Must deep within her clearly be his equal,

Her sensibility glorious as his plumage.
Could it be so? That dull drab miserable bird?
We viewed her with new respect; we paid due homage;
But sometimes thought, whatever part she had played
In bringing that blazing splendour out of the dark,
Some utterly unknown principle was at work.

TWO ENGLISHMEN

Far, far from home they rode on their excursions
And looked with much amusement and compassion
On Indians and Africans and Persians,
People indeed of any foreign nation
Who milled in mobs completely uninhibited
In the peculiar lands that they inhabited.

But in their own small island crowded thickly,
Each with his pride of self and race and caste,
They could not help but be a little prickly
And in their wisdom they evolved at last
This simple code to save them from destruction—
One did not speak without an introduction.

So naturally when Kinglake on his camel,
Mounted aloft to see the world or take it,
Saw faint against the sky's hard blue enamel
A solar topee, then a shooting jacket,
Then all too clear an Englishman appearing
He found the prospect anything but cheering.

Merely because the distances were wider
One could not speak with every Dick or Harry,
For all he knew some absolute outsider,
Who trotted up upon his dromedary,
And yet he felt, alone and unprotected
On these bare sands some talk might be expected.

Of course, he thought, with spirits briefly lightened,
Though ten to one he did not know the fellow
He might be quite all right; but then he mightn't;
And on he came by sandy hill and hollow—
It was a bit too thick thus to arrive at
The desert's core and then not find it private.

For if for one's own reasons one had ridden
By camel through the empty wastes to Cairo
From Gaza in the distance back there hidden
One did not do the thing to play the hero
Or have some chap come dropping from the sky
To ask what one was doing there, and why.

The sweat lay on his camel dank and soapy
And Kinglake too broke out in perspiration
For close and closer in his solar topee
The stranger came with steady undulation;
One could not hide, for shelter there was none,
Nor yet, however tempting, cut and run.

No, if they met, as meet it seemed they must,
Though heartily he wished him at the devil,
Kinglake decided, halting in the dust,
That if the fellow spoke he must be civil;
But then observed, in ultimate dismay,
He could not think of anything to say.

But he, as it fell out, need not have worried.
It was an English military man
Long years in Burma boiled, in India curried,
Who riding home on some deep private plan
Now sat his camel equally embarrassed
To find himself thus hunted out and harassed;

And while their Arab servants rushed together
With leaps and yells to suit the glad occasion
Each Englishman gazed coolly at the other
And briefly touched his hat in salutation
And so passed by, erect, superb, absurd,
Across the desert sands without a word.

But when they'd passed, one gesture yet endures;
Each turned and waved his hand as if to say,
"Well, help yourself to Egypt"—"India's yours,"
And so continued grandly on his way;
And as they went, one feels that, truth to tell,
They understood each other pretty well.

REFLECTIONS AT A PARKING METER

One knew men changed. It was of course notorious
When drums and trumpets sounded war's first rumour
That men became the drums; or still more glorious
Dissolved into a hollow suit of armour
And so transfigured, bronze and fierce and furious,
Hacked each other to pieces without a tremor.

In peacetime too, at least upon occasion,
We saw they took an equally strange course:
All vehicles that galloped to collision,
All citizens run down without remorse,
Proved that mankind, perceived in proper vision,
Became at times a chariot or a horse.

One might have thought, since man had this propensity
For taking on the force if not appearance
Of anything he rode with such intensity,
When Stephenson invented railway engines
We would be filled right up with their immensity
And thunder down the highroads with a vengeance;

But trains by a most merciful dispensation
Lived in some hell contrived for them alone
Locked in their smoke from station straight to station,
Controlled by one black demon on his throne;
Therefore the passengers knew no temptation.
The effect on engine drivers remains unknown.

Yet maddened with their might and their persistence
Small boys were changed to trains before our eyes.
Bursting with fire and smoke and pounding pistons,
All locomotives in spirit if not in size,
They charged away and vanished in the distance;
So that what happened next should not surprise.

For once we had the car from the inventor,
The horseless carriage, then the swift tin lizzie,
Man made it, we could see, his only mentor.
There was no harm at first, the pace was easy,
The man and car joined calmly like a centaur;
But soon, as we know well, the roads went crazy.

Some saw the true position quite reversed;
The car, they said, was just a starter button
That loosed man's own fierce passions at their worst;
Fired with the chance it gave he stamped his foot on
His own accelerator in a burst
That knocked his fellows down like so much mutton.

But was this so? When walking or commuting
People were still humane in act and speech:
They could converse together without tooting,
They did not walk at sixty m.p.h.;
They moved through crowded streets without disputing,
And if they bumped, begged pardon each to each.

They did not fail to cherish their domestics,
Their cats, their dogs, their neighbours near and far:
How could they lose all human characteristics
The moment they sat down to drive a car,
And fill the press with casualty statistics
Far worse though less dramatic than in war?

There was but one true answer to the question:
Man was not wicked but his will was weak,
His mind was far too open to suggestion;
And when we filled him like a hollow tank
With power and speed and petrol in combustion
He *was* the car he drove, or so to speak.

Cars had no brains at all beneath the bonnet,
They had one driving will to go go go,
The road was theirs and while their wheels were on it
Nothing must make them turn aside or slow;
They burnt their lives out at a mile a minute;
And man, being one with them, behaved just so.

He was a kind of motive apparatus
Fixed in its place behind the steering wheel;
And, filled with his mechanical afflatus,
He could not pause, he could not think or feel.
With eyes like glaring headlamps he came at us,
The metal man, the human automobile.

To go go go became his natural function:
So cars met cars, there was no real driver,
And crashed on curves and bumped at each road junction;
Cars cursed at cars and knocked each other over,
Cars pushed through city crowds without compunction.
The wonder is that there was one survivor.

And as the cars rode shining to their fate
Quite unaware of it and their condition,
Spurning the road beneath their rubber feet,
All men bowed down to them with strange submission;
We ran to please them for they could not wait,
We leapt, we lived, we died by their permission.

Some thought we could escape from this anomaly
By preaching to the young. But if they heard,
The young were not impressed by moral homily;
And since their dads were cars, and cars their lord,
It seemed each hopeful member of the family
Was born to be a Holden or a Ford.

Faintly one hoped that man might make a car
More sympathetic to his best intentions;
A courteous car, a shy car like a deer,
A car that shrank from violence and dissensions,
A sensitive car, a car that could not bear
The sights upon the road that no one mentions.

Meantime in truth it was no laughing matter,
The traffic rushed and crashed without abatement
And man was great on earth but cars were greater.
Wherefore the poet, troubled by such treatment,
Has paused in protest by a parking meter
And switched his engine off to make this statement.

FOUR-LETTER WORDS

Rejoice, all souls, I sing four-letter words,
One two three four, it is the mystic number,
None gives such pleasure as a four affords,
None stands so firm; so therefore we remember
Miss Pimm, Professor Ink, and all who latterly
Fought in the courts for four and *Lady Chatterley*.

How ludicrous it was, they argued rightly,
That five and six were always neat and clean
And you could say the strangest things politely
In synonyms of twelve or seventeen
While fours could get you jailed in conversation
Or if in print would startle the whole nation.

True the particular fours they had in mind
Were a rude Anglo-Saxon sort of noise,
For older times and rougher ways designed,
Not suitable for little girls and boys;
They seldom dropped them at the dinner table
But kept them for the pigsty or the stable.

But they were not concerned to hear them spoken,
They stood against the censorship of letters.
Should publishers be fined and authors broken
And the white Muse herself stand bound in fetters
Because they used four signs instead of three?
Were we to keep on banning *Lady C.*?

And if the words contained some impropriety
They merely told of some small natural functions
More plainly than was usual in society,
Some brief appendages and odd conjunctions
Of man and woman joined like cup and saucer,
And all were found in Rabelais and Chaucer.

How rich they glowed in those old royal sinners,
How they lit up the age-old human comedy
Like wine and mustard with their roast-beef dinners.
Our age was faint and pale: here lay the remedy,
Let the four-letter words pour out in torrents
Or cease, at least, to pester D. H. Lawrence.

Did we not reach the height of the absurd
When we could print the male for fowl or parrot
While if we used the self-same little word
To mean that amiable object like a carrot
The fat was in the fire and no mistake?
Could we not name a spade or use a rake?

This was an outrage to all human reason,
This was the death of truth, the slough of wit,
So off to court—the court was in vacation—
So off to court, when it came back to sit
Strode bold Professor Ink, and after him,
With many more, the valiant Miss Pimm.

There was a word they'd never dreamed of uttering,
Its letters reached the mystic total four.
Could they refrain when freedom's lamp was guttering
And one small breath would blow it bright once more?
While judges quailed and pressmen blessed their luck
Each one in turn pronounced the brave word ———.

They said it once they said it twice and thrice,
They jumped for joy, they made the welkin ring,
It sounded queer, it sounded rather nice;
And, what was the extraordinary thing,
In town or village, bathroom, church or bed,
All over England not a soul dropped dead.

And round the world the glorious news was rung
For though in swamps like Eire or Australia
Some fogs of ancient prejudice still clung,
The law proclaimed in pomp and full regalia
That books could now be printed, poems sung
In words direct and down to earth as dung.

Ah poor Miss Pimm and brave Professor Ink,
After a victory comes its aftermath.
On second thoughts, had they but paused to think,
Did lovers wandering down the garden path
Wish to converse in words so really awful;
And would they be such fun now they were lawful?

Shut in their libraries and calmly reading
They'd noticed some odd things but not the oddest,
Which was that when it came to actual breeding
Nature herself thought wisest to be modest;
Though she had put great pleasure in that spot
She thought when asked to face it, one might not.

With flowers, with fur, with feathers she diverted
Attention from the parts she thought uncouth;
With honey scent, with coy retreat she flirted
And never once revealed the naked truth,
Far less discussed in words the curious capers
Performed, so it is said, by stout gamekeepers.

How chastely stands the mare in the green pasture,
Her flowing tail concealing what's forbidden;
Even the stallion takes a modest posture
And keeps his mighty engine mostly hidden;
Only one creature strayed from Nature's plan,
And that was that ambitious biped man.

For when he stood up straight in evolution
And lost his fur, his shielding flanks, his tail,
We found him clad in nothing but confusion;
And that is why, since Nature must prevail,
He rushed to trousers, petticoat or pinny,
Fig-leaf, grass skirt, at least to a bikini;

And that is why, of course, when books were printed
He ran like mad from the four-letter word,
Though well content its import should be hinted.
All men wore clothes, most truly he averred,
In farms and towns, in palaces and hovels,
Yet still we stripped him naked in our novels.

What follows then when Pimm that dear good creature
And headlong Ink have leapt the age-old fences
And flown full tilt against the face of Nature?
Why, two quite unexpected consequences:
For first, no novelist can now be daring
And what is worse, they have abolished swearing.

For though concerned with truth in all its clarity
And claiming the whole human field as tillable,
Writers enjoyed a skirmish with authority
And finding some ingenious monosyllable
That meant the worst just suitably diminished:
What could they write, now all that fun was finished?

And as for swearing, can we bear its loss?
For there are times we must have Anglo-Saxon.
How can you muster sheep, describe the boss,
Or drive a car through any intersection
Without a stock of quite unprintable curses?
The editor who dares reject your verses,

The critic who condemns, if one can't call him
A simple ———, or shatter his serenity
By wishing that the bluntest fate befall him
And have it ring with decent deep obscenity,
What use are things? If all the words are seen
In open print, what's left to be obscene?

And finally if we bared ourselves in books
Was not the next step bare the person too?
Then would we thus confronted with our looks
And what we were, and what we had to do,
Decide appalled we'd better do without it?
Would mankind perish? Frankly, then, I doubt it.

For novelists were far too fond of scribbling
And men of love and its attendant scandals
To let all wicked words thus cease from troubling
And, so to speak, completely drop their bundles.
Never would they agree a court had docked them
Of their old right of peeping at what shocked them.

They would invent some new five-letter word
For any rude protuberance or cavity
Or find some synonym to be abhorred
Not noticed heretofore with proper gravity;
Or best of all in this absurd position
Quite simply disregard the court's decision.

So after all raise up the solemn anthem
For Pimm and Ink and all their bold array;
They really did no harm, all men must grant them,
They cleared the path for some new Rabelais.
And but for their brave stand in far-off Britain
This poem, save the mark, had not been written.

FAREWELL TO JINDABYNE

Let us lament for Jindabyne, it is going to be drowned,
Let us shed tears, as many as the occasion warrants;
The Snowy, the Thredbo and the Eucumbene engulf it,
Combining their copious torrents.

Progress of course is necessary, progress is admirable,
But let us not march to the future without due charity;
Pray for poor Jindabyne gripped in the steely fingers
Of the Snowy Mountains Authority.

True, many a time imprisoned in this hot pocket
While oily men in overalls, powerful and easy,
Banged at some client's tractor, ignoring the anguish
Of stranger's engine or chassis,

Many a time thus freed in a cloud of flies
To contemplate all that Jindabyne has to offer
Awake or asleep in its hollow between the hills
And the somewhat polluted river—

The scars of snow still gleaming on blue Kosciusko,
The caravan camp where citizens far from home
Daring the dangerous mountains but taking no chances
Crowd in a comforting slum,

The souvenir shop with its stuffed koala bears
(Not manufactured in any local forest),
The two small cafés, the three enormous garages
Serving the hasting tourist,

The acres of junkyard where mangled and rusting cars
Dwindling to meet the river with other effluvia
Bear witness to mighty sprees of the lonely workers
From Poland and Yugoslavia,

The dust and the glare and the stifling lifeless air,
The ancient and ruinous shacks where those who have chosen
To live in Jindabyne do, in summer baked,
In the long winter frozen—

Many a time thus viewing the total township
And thinking how soon it was all to be buried in water
Like drowned Atlantis and never be heard of again,
I have thought: the sooner the better.

It is a town, one feels, that foresaw its doom;
Nothing, except the hotel, was built for permanence;
And over the fibro, the weatherboard and corrugated iron,
Crowding each rocky eminence

The green wild briars march down like an army of outlaws
That, armed with its thorns, with banners of blossom gladdened,
In one last leap from the hills would have taken it soon
If the clean bright water hadn't.

But let us not therefore refrain from lamentation.
Surely one mourns when a town goes under the water?
Surely there are secret charms, there are virtues in Jindabyne
Concealed from a mere outsider?

What will become of Hans at the Kookaburra Café
When water has wetted the salad and soaked the chop?
What will become of Rankin's and Jindabyne Motors,
Ivan J. Williams, Prop.?

Shall the eligible maiden behind the milkbar counter
Be eligible only to eels? Shall Leo A. Hore
In the wooden annexe to the pub be licensed to sell
Spirituous liquors no more?

I fear for the lean grey cat that lurks near the butcher's,
And the bantam hen and her six Black Orpington chickens,
And the fox and the rabbits at play among the rocks
All covered with grey-green lichens.

I fear for the General Store; I fear for E. Kluger:
Shall he be sunk with his famous salami sausages?
I fear for the old folk peering like bony goannas
Out of the doors of their cottages.

Rest. Be at peace. There is nothing to weep for here.
The rabbits will prudently retreat before the waters.
Benevolent authority will remove the ancient inhabitants,
Their cats and their sons and daughters.

Already New Jindabyne, shining with modern amenities,
Astonishes the Hereford cattle on higher ground,
From where like uncomfortable eagles the old folks shall stare
Down on their nests that are drowned.

They shall have new brick bungalows, electric stoves,
Refrigerators, toilets, more than they dreamed or wished;
How can we make lamentation when the whole town
Is raised up, purified, washed?

Yet something still lingers in Jindabyne, something that walks,
While the cat's fur stands on end and the kelpie whines,
With a cobwebbed beard around the old pisé hotel
In the shade of its towering pines.

Shall we make lament for the far brave pioneers?
Gold-rush? Stage-coach? Cattle brought down from the snow?
Whatever it was that walked in Jindabyne
It died too long ago,

And left no more for the water to cover now
Than a vague sense of some purpose gone to waste
And, lingering still with the ghosts in the old hotel,
A steadfast, abiding thirst.

Let us not weep at all, then, let us rejoice
With a suitable noise like turbines, silently humming;
Whether it thirsts for purpose or merely for liquid
Jindabyne now is brimming;

Straight through the mountains marches the S.M.A.,
Sparkling with light and pouring with irrigation,
And down go the towns in its path and up go the pylons,
And a great deal of good to the nation.

But still while progress and water advance on the town
And the dams fill high, yes even while we rejoice,
Jindabyne calls us, for reasons best known to itself,
In a very small wet voice.

And so for the far brave beards of the pioneers
For the old hotel and the pine tree drowned for ever,
For someone who once was young here and once made love
On the banks of the Snowy River,

For something still fainter and far away back in time,
The shy dark shadowy aboriginal race
Always like creatures in water, who left one word
And melted without a trace,

Or finally for the mystery and the pathos
That seep from earth and bubble out from water
In any place where men have lived and bred
And feuded with each other,

Let one dim bell, from either of the rival churches,
When deep lie the spires in water and deep the pine,
Sometimes be heard on soft warm summer evenings
Lamenting Jindabyne.

WASP

Well wasp what's
To do about you
Battering at the windscreen
You can't get through?

World's all wrong,
Air itself in treason
Suddenly turns solid
And shuts you in prison.

And still through the wall wasp
The long green paddocks sweeten
With trigger-flower and daisy
And gold billy-button;

But up wasp down wasp
Climb wasp and fall,
Can't beat your way
Through the clear strange wall.

Out and away then
When the car stops;
World's come right again
And happy goes wasp.

BLOWAWAY GRASS

There she goes flying
Like straw alas
My blowaway girl
In the blowaway grass.

We should have known
We knew too well
There is no holding
A blowaway girl

But so many pretty things
Came to pass
When we sat down
In the blowaway grass

Where it shone so warm
Like silk of the sun
Over the hot wild
Gully of stone

And covered the granite's
Knuckle and chink
Piling so soft
Where the briar bloomed pink

We both forgot
Or pretended to
How the world must roll
When the next wind blew.

The wind blows high
From gully to hill
And there you go flying
My blowaway girl

While your poor lover
Alone alas
Sits chewing a straw
In the blowaway grass.

EARLY

Sometimes these autumn mornings when mists unfurl
Grey waters flushing and gleaming with rose and pearl
A single clang of iron in the distance sounds,
And we know it is man out there, moving so early.
Then in this soft obscurity while we see clearly,
Like the first man on earth how strangely he stands
Alive in the mist there, sounding his iron chime
While out of nowhere, out of what ages of time
All round him flows as it has flowed for ever
Gleaming with rose and pearl the silent water.

THE MICE OF CHINKAPOOK

In summer when the sun was warm
Shaw Neilson rode around the farm
And in his mind like some clear spring
Soft words and tunes began to sing.
He wrote them down in his notebook
To keep them safe, and feared no harm
From men or mice at Chinkapook.

He watched the bright blue dragonfly,
He saw the skylark climb the sky,
He heard around his pony's knees
The grasshoppers clap the yellow breeze,
And sometimes in a tussocky nook
Like silver water hurrying by
He saw the mice of Chinkapook.

The swarming mice, the hungry mice,
Their teeth were sharp and white and fierce,
They bit their way through field and crop,
They ate the haystack to its top,
They crept into the house and took
The poet's notebook slice by slice,
The nibbling mice of Chinkapook.

Oh what was that strange taste they knew
As through the notebook chew by chew
In moonlight when the house was still
Those wicked creatures ate their fill?
Perhaps it burnt, perhaps it shook
Like sunlight in a drop of dew
The lucky mice of Chinkapook.

You'd think that when they'd fed enough
On what that notebook tasted of,
The strawberries and oranges,
And bluebells under honey trees,
And mushrooms with their elfin look—
Such magic as must surely move
Even the mice of Chinkapook—

Transfigured mice they would have run,
Like jewels in the moon or sun.—
It may be so, but no one hears
Of emerald mice with diamond ears;
They can't be found by hook or crook
But did their deed and then ran on
With what they stole from Chinkapook.

Well, mice are small and mice must live
But when you think of all that love
Of brightness flashing from the dim
Of night and earth and water's brim
That sang for joy in that lost book,
Only Shaw Neilson could forgive
The thieving mice of Chinkapook.

ANTS

Who lifted that stone off our nest?
The city is all laid bare.
Fierce light leaps in like a beast,
All run, some here, some there.

Oh who could have lifted stone?
What monstrous jaw, what shoulder,
To tug until stone quite gone,
To heave the world's great boulder?

208

But stone that was rafter, was roof,
Covering the life of the swarm,
Good stone, kind stone, safe,
Protector from raider, from storm,

Stone we have touched, we have known,
And set in his place for ever,
Big noble beautiful stone,
Not possible to turn him over.

Oh stone our strength in battle,
Oh stone our earth and our sky,
Flat on your back like a beetle
Quite overturned you lie.

Who turned great stone on his back?
Who did the deed to our king?
All soldiers rush out to attack
But cannot see whom to sting.

Big tall invisible ones
Shadows of terror and doubt
Or small ones, stealers of stones,
Encompass us all about.

Oh in stone's speechlessness
What to do now, where go?
All in too much distress
Run here, run to and fro.

· · · · ·

Well then it's time for shifting,
Come soldier, come worker, come nurse;
But pardon, my brothers, for lifting
The lid of your universe.

D'ALBERTIS

D'Albertis with his smoking gun
While all New Guinea rang with thunder
Through fern and bush came crashing down
Half filled with triumph, half with wonder.
The grass grew soft in the green glade,
The little stream ran clear and sweet,
And suddenly he stopped dismayed
To see it struggling at his feet—

The bird he'd watched one moment since
And heard its deep wild challenge sound,
Ruffling like some barbaric prince
Proud and secure on its own ground,
The cloak of velvet shot with green,
The dancing head-dress bright as ice,
The shining black, the emerald sheen,
The six-plumed bird of paradise.

Hunted so long and prized so much!
Now struck to that dark struggling shape—
He could not stretch his hand to touch,
He could not stoop to pick it up,
But huge and silently he stood
Transfixed by absolute remorse
While shadows prowled through grass and wood
And sunlight burned him like a curse.

No casuistry, no excuse
Could speak for man, he thought; and then,
What if the deed had been no use?
What profit to himself or men
If pierced by arrows, burned by fever,
He fell where no one ever found him
As well he might, up some dark river,
With all his futile trophies round him?

But then, D'Albertis being man,
And strong and bearded and immense,
The age-old casuistries began
Or were they reason and plain sense?—
For he this day was full of life
And if the bird was dead, it was,
Too far for reach of pain or grief
As now he took it from the grass.

Some force too deep to understand,
The love of what was rare and strange,
The thrust of nations to expand,
The strong man's call to rove and range,
The restless and inquiring mind
That drove mankind from its dim birth,
The over-mastering need to find
All secrets of our home, the earth,

Had brought him out to this far land,
And if this bird of velvet flame
Glinting and sparkling in his hand
With silver ruff and showering plume
Had paid for man that fatal price
At least he too and with a will
Would make the same last sacrifice
If the dark land moved in to kill.

Surely New Guinea from its wealth
Of curious flower and exquisite bird
That shone in mist and flew in stealth
Unseen by man, unknown, unheard,
Could spare this single specimen
That in some far museum yet
Should live its glimmering life for men
Of joy and wonder and regret?

He could not feel the deed was good,
But through the jungle to his camp
In gathering dusk D'Albertis strode,
And there beside his lonely lamp
He took the skin to show to men
And then with heart and mind at peace
Like some black lion in its den
He ate the bird of paradise.

MUNGO PARK

Sir Walter Scott once chanced on Mungo Park
Tossing wee bits of pebbles in the burn.
"Well Mungo, man, but this is idle work,
To see you lost in mist and rock and fern
After the far wild things you've seen and done
With nought to do but play with stones and water."
But Mungo laughed, and tossed another stone
And watched it sinking. "Not quite so, Sir Walter—

"Do you not see those five small crystal bubbles
That like the buds of flowers come welling up?
That is because there's air around my pebbles
Which takes a certain time to reach the top.
Now toss a stone and watch the bubbles flower
And think we have to cross some unknown stream;
If they come quick we'll make it, if they're slower
Why then we'll drown no doubt if we can't swim.

"Sometimes I like to practise this small knack.
In Africa when I was on my travels—"
"Oh man alive, I think you're going back.
I dinna like your game with stones and bubbles
For it's yourself you toss into the dark.
And where to now?" "Where else but to the Niger?"
"Not there of all earth's places, Mungo Park!
You've seen it, man; go find some safer river."

"Aye once at Segu in the morning's dazzle
Through the tall reeds I saw the Niger flowing;
But flowing where, Sir Walter, that's the puzzle?
If it goes east, as I have seen it going,
It seeps into the desert to be burned
And that's the end of that; but if at last
When one had followed far enough it turned
Westward through unknown country to the coast—"

"To Segu, then, where you have been before
And learnt how it would crush you blow by blow:
Four months a prisoner of the barbarous Moor
Who kept you like a circus beast for show,
Spat upon, beaten, starved, reviled and hated,
Mocked by the women, racked by fear and fever,
Kept half alive for sport while they debated
How soon they'd kill the dog of an unbeliever,

"And when by miracle you escaped that night
And in the storm the lightning flash revealed
The horseman in his solitary flight,
Your clothes in rags, your hair and beard gone wild,
Your youth and strength all wasted down to bones,
With nothing but your compass and your horse—
Floundering through bogs and stumbling over stones—
And your great will to take you on your course—

"Why then when you had come to that last plain
Where lions roared and rivers raged in flood
There on a lonely hilltop in the rain
Waiting like fate the three tall horsemen stood;
And stripped you bare, horse, money, food and gun,
And spared your life but left you there a prey
For savage beasts and still more savage men,
Alone and naked, friendless in Africa."

"Yet the sun shone; and one day's march ahead
I saw the Niger roll; and here I am."
"Aye, and came back to us as one long dead
To find the whole world ringing with your name.
What need's for more than that?" "Why it must jingle
A second time, and never mind the price,
For I am for the Niger and the jungle."
"Ye canna hope to have the same luck twice."

"Shall I live here a medico in Peebles
With petty sickness like a lame dog whining
Or by the burn-side sit and play with pebbles
When I have seen the broad blue river shining
And put my strength against the whole dark land?
Suppose I know the risk—Sir Walter, look,
For what it costs in cramp of mind or hand
Would you not turn to write another book?"

"Oh aye, I'd write. But what's it count to scribble?"
"There's those have passed by night at Abbotsford
And seen your shadow huge like your great double
Hunched in your lonely struggle with the word
And watched your hand in your dim candle's lighting
Fly on your window blind like some dark bird
All through the midnight, writing, writing, writing,
And marvelled that you drove yourself so hard."

"Aye then I've worked an hour or two to paint
The heath, the rocks, the men of my own country
And when the cocks crew and the light came faint
And still I watched there like some weary sentry
Have felt if truth be known I'd tried my power
Right to the utmost limit of my tether
And then beyond; yet to my dying hour
Hope in my hand to fly the grey goose feather.

214

"But man it's still a pettifogging trade.
Here I sit safe at home and drive my pen
Or limp a mile to find my pine-trees' shade
And watch the burn come bubbling down the glen,
While you will face the desert's lion glare
And see the Niger roll at Bamako
And on into the jungle, God knows where—
Aye, Mungo, man, and would that I could go!"

"Each to his trade, and mine's to walk, Sir Walter;
Yet in the countries never seen by men
Who's paid the greater price, who's gone the further,
I with my travels, you with your midnight pen?
My road lies far; yet it could be, my friend,
In mile and mile we go or book and book
We take the same strange journey in the end.
What can we do but wish each other luck?"

Then up the misty hill they rode together.
"I dinna trust your luck," Sir Walter said
When Mungo's horse lost footing in the heather.
But Mungo laughed and rode on straight ahead.
"We'll smile at that," he said, "when I get back,"
And parted so, as it turned out for ever,
Sir Walter to his candle and his book
And Mungo to the light on his blue river.

FORMIGA DE FOGO

Bates with his stinging rifle,
Mysteriously impelled
To march and suffer and stifle
Collecting birds and monkeys
In the Amazonian jungle,

Was much amused, so he said,
When far up the river at Aveyros,
That wretched village in the mud,
The natives told him their story
Of ants that were born of blood.

It seemed this poor simple people,
True fruits of the tropic land,
Peaceful and naked and idle,
Who dozed all day in their hammocks,
Subsisting mainly on turtle,

Had lately been driven so wild
By armies of stinging ants
Swarming in street and field
They had fled in dismay from the village,
Man and woman and child.

This was the ant of fire
The terrible formiga de fogo
Not known in these parts before
Though they had crept through the jungle
Closer each year by year.

And well in amazement and terror
Might the poor natives run,
For when the ant-heaps boiled over
Foraging, hungry for land,
And sent their scouts up the river

And found some suitable home
Where men had made a clearing,
Then in their thousands they came
Like a shudder of sparks through the jungle,
Like a red stream of flame,

And in their phalanxes packed
Like a war of red-hot needles
They bit and stung and attacked
Till they made the place untenable
In plain incredible fact.

And because the village by the water
In the year before they came
Had known a far worse invader
Who filled their drowsy streets
With fire and pain and slaughter,

These simple villagers said
Formiga de fogo were born
Of drops of burning blood
Which where some few were wounded
The fierce Cabanas shed.

So far as he records
It is not known if Bates
Harmlessly killing birds
So many miles from England
Thought long on these wild words:

Who the Cabanas were;
How cruel they must have been,
Filling the night with fear,
That men could come to believe
They bled this stinging fire;

And whether all war was not,
As in their dim perception
The natives almost thought,
The ant-heap blindly boiling
After the first brave scout. . . .

As a small pleasing trifle
He noted the superstition
And with his stinging rifle,
Foraging for birds and monkeys,
Strode on into the jungle.

TE RAUPARAHA

Wicked bold deeds are remembered: why?
The stone and the water sleep in peace
And have no notion they saw men die
Once in the dawn on Onawe ridge;
But the wave hits the rock, aha, aha,
And we remember Te Rauparaha.

We have forgotten so much else
But something about that bloody old chieftain,
Devious, murderous, cruel, false,
Stirs in the mind obscure and uncertain,
Calls up his shadow against our will
Dark over Akaroa still.

For great ambition moved this man
And great inhuman ruthlessness.
Village by village, clan by clan,
The Maoris lived in war and peace
But Rauparaha, aha, aha,
Bought muskets from the pakeha.

Bright with laughter, black with anger,
Filled with one single burning thought
To loot, to kill, to drive, to conquer,
He led his swarming tribesmen out;
From Kawhia to Kapiti
His dark canoes were over the sea.

Were they not wicked those pakeha
Who bought his flax and sold him guns?
He swept the coastline pa by pa
And they who were the strong men once,
Wicked enough but not enough,
Rot in the sea with time's dead stuff.

But this was a man to conquer worlds,
Or a whole island, two islands now,
For over the strait's grey stormy wilds
The greenstone mountains shone in their snow
And out from Kapiti rocking south
Te Rauparaha came with his greedy mouth.

"Why should he come, we have done no harm,
He has his lands, we have ours;
One green ridge we have for our home
And the little waves break on it like flowers."
Kaiapoi said in a voice like doom
Te Rauparaha has come, has come.

There at the gates of Onawe pa
(Come by stealth and strike them early)
Silent stood Te Rauparaha;
Some cried flight and some cried parley—
This was the moment Te Rauparaha
Had waited for, aha, aha.

Death at Onawe and all soon over;
Deep in the green anonymous water
Round the low ridge at Akaroa
The lost ones lie who were put to slaughter;
And when the wave cries, one man still
Walks in my mind against my will:

Tall, hawk-faced, savage, half-naked,
Yet in inhuman cold and heat
As cruel and bold and great and wicked
As conquerors we've marvelled at
In civilized places far from here
Who tore green Europe up with war—

Te Rauparaha who saw so clearly
His mission was to conquer and kill
With no pretence at dealing fairly
And no excuse but his own will
And with surprise, aha, aha
In the muskets from the pakeha.

When he was old and walked his village
With shrunken body like an ape's
And no more power to kill and ravage
He turned a Christian man—perhaps!
But in his talk, the bishop grieved,
Still burned the battles he had loved.

Nobody knew his secret mind,
They only knew that once he stood
The master of the whole green land,
That all his days he dealt in blood
And watched with bright and pitiless eye
His enemies and his followers die.

Dark days, go under the ground;
Dark chief, at Otaki sleep;
Yet still that question troubles my mind
I neither can answer nor escape:
Soft green sea and clear blue sky
But wicked bold deeds are remembered . . . why?

THE LOST REEF

And came again as though he were fated
To that same sudden rocky hill
From where he had seen as if foretold
One shining mile of solid gold
Where the next ridge before him rolled
And stood still
And gesticulated.

Twenty years it had shone and waited
Since first he found it by his skill
And turned exhausted down the track;
But it was his to touch and take
And his alone as he came back
And stood still
And gesticulated.

"Some said I dreamed, some said I cheated
Or boasted for some wicked thrill—
I laughed at that, but if some thief
Should stumble on and steal my reef
I should go mad with rage and grief,"
And stood still
And gesticulated.

"My friends dropped out, dismayed, defeated,
The bearded dragon shook its frill
And mocked me with its gaping grin
But on across the iron plain
I strode to find my gold again,"
And stood still
And gesticulated.

So now once more he stood elated
In that hot wind and drank his fill
And stared around him from the crest
North and south and east and west
And so much horror pierced his breast
He stood still
And gesticulated.

Naked as Adam first created
With their long spears held high to kill
Like shadows out of the shadowless ground
The tall lean black men gathered round
And stood amazed as with no sound
He stood still
And gesticulated.

"But it was here I laughed and sweated
And watched that mile of gold distil
Its yellow light on the bright air.
And where it glittered high and clear
The plain before me all lies bare,"
And stood still
And gesticulated.

"Then simply is my problem stated,
It seems I came to the wrong hill
So now must pause to eat and rest
And then set out to east or west
Or north or south as seems the best,"
And stood still
And gesticulated.

The black men much commiserated
To see him lie so weak and ill,
They wished that they could understand
What thing it was in their hot land
He clutched at in his empty hand,
And stood still
And gesticulated.

And when they brought him food he ate it,
Took water in his mouth to swill,
And should he sleep or should he rave
They watched in awe around his cave
To see how white men should behave
And stood still
And gesticulated.

"I stand with ardour unabated,
I lack no strength of body or will;
There is a mile of gold I know
But when I move to that bright glow
I do not know which way to go,"
And stood still
And gesticulated.

The curst mirage equivocated
And filled his mind with icy chill
And where the tide of silver flame
All round him flowed, each way the same,
The whole world floated like a dream
And stood still
And gesticulated.

"One thought is not to be tolerated
That when I saw that white ridge spill
Its yellow treasure for me to find
The sun had made me crazed and blind
And all I saw was my own mind,"
And stood still
And gesticulated.

"I have been feasted, I have been feted,
I have great promises to fulfil,
And I have told all men the truth
For that great light I saw in youth
Still surely glitters north or south,"
And stood still
And gesticulated.

"The sun glares down as though he hated,
The eagle cries out high and shrill,
But there is some magnetic force
That's led me straight upon my course
Through country wild as this and worse,"
And stood still
And gesticulated.

"Far too long I have hesitated
And turned all ways, a mere windmill;
If I could start, if I could put
Either my right or my left foot
On any track I would set out,"
And stood still
And gesticulated.

The blacks stole off while he debated
But often they looked back until
Like some far shrunken skeleton
Alone upon his knoll of stone
He melted into the yellow sun
And stood still
And gesticulated.

THE CHAIR

I knew a man so old he was like an angel,
Light so consumed him he glittered as frail as crystal;

And as he lay on his pillow in his white hair
He fixed his blue eyes on an object, and it was a chair.

But was it a chair? It was so strange a shape
He thought he had dragged it over the edge of sleep.

It seemed to waver, it was all hollows and space,
It was hardly there, and yet beyond doubt it was.

See it had legs, one two, yes, three and four,
Rounded and tapered, so delicately set on the floor;

And round the legs ran a rung in a pretty ring
He touched it in thought like a harper touching a string.

Oh it was a chair all right, there was the seat
In its dainty circle, waiting for someone to sit;

How perfectly shaped it was for sitting upon,
Like a saddle on a little horse, but the horse was gone.

And when he thought of all who had sat in that chair,
The beautiful ladies, the children floating in air,

And elephants hauling its timber in misty greenery
And sawmills ringing with their singing keen machinery,

And the chairs before it, right back to when chairs began
Far in dim time past Sheraton and Queen Anne,

That lovely procession of chairs, with people sitting
Or about to sit, and smiling and fading and flitting,

How wonderful it was to lie in the universe
Where of all lucky things men had made chairs.

To look at a chair and see it look back at him squarely—
Oh why had he never observed a chair so clearly?

He must own a hundred himself, at any rate fifty,
Kitchen and dining and drawing room, one for the baby—

When he got home he would touch them one by one,
He would notice each chair before he dared to sit down;

He wished he had noticed them before, but here they all were
Melting together, merged in this single chair.

It seemed to move, but did it? No, it stayed put,
So lightly touching the floor with each exquisite foot.

What craftsman had made it for him with plane and with chisel
And built it so fine that now it was floating a little

So that alone in space it had its strange being
Down that long tunnel of light at the end of his seeing—

Oh high in that crystal dazzle shining it stood
Carved upon space, that queer sweet shape of wood,

Far and so clear . . . I had another old friend
Who said to me once when he knew he was near his end,

"I am not afraid of death, but how will it come?"
And I could have said but embarrassment struck me dumb:

"I knew a man who died without fear or care
In absolute ecstacy, thinking about a chair."

CAVE PAINTING

Look there are dark hands in the black rock,
Man's hands, woman's hands, child's hands hiding in a cave,
Shadows of hands, but with such a living look
They seem to waver and beckon, they seem to move
In a language of gesture startling and piercing as speech.
Up from the green water here we clambered
Say the hands and the bodies of the hands, to hold and to touch,
And here we camped, and here we shall be remembered.

And they are so close and yet so far and wild
They seem to breathe and speak for all humanity
Who made their camp so, man and woman and child,
And flowed with the green river down to infinity;
And beautifully and terribly they wave
In the black rock, like hands alive in a grave.

GRANITE

Grey outcrops of granite
Please me much because
I see this old planet
Has bones under its grass.

And balancing one on the other
With such surprising agility
Or huddling like sheep together
They have a strange look of fertility

As if the bare earth at least
Whatever else was done
By flower or man or beast
Could grow a fine crop of stone.

But they are not merely mineral,
They are a kind of altar
Where anything, plant or animal,
Hunted, can come for shelter.

Bacon-and-eggs that fears
To have its head bitten off
Fans out its golden flowers
Low on the rock and is safe.

Thornbush believing darkly
All creatures are its enemies
Squats here stubborn and prickly
Baring its fangs in the crevices.

Out of the dangerous paddock
Of mattock and poison the briar
Hangs up like notes of music
Its berries of clear red fire;

And fierce as briar and thornbush
In deeper dark recesses
The copperhead coils in ambush,
The blue-tongued lizard hisses.

I give the flickering rabbit
Credit for one firm thought
That here in a hole under granite
No one can dig him out.

I see with equal pleasure
The grey rock polished with wool
Where sheep have crowded from the weather
Against the lee-side wall.

But sometimes tall in the paddocks
At noon or looming dusk
When the stones are deep with shadows
And the rock smells wild with fox

They seem no mere haven
For sheep and the hunted ones
But stand up brooding to heaven
Like stones men worshipped once,

And seem so old and so stable
One can lay hands on them
And touch in each grey bubble
Cool everlasting time.

I have stretched out my hand
Or bent my forehead down
Seeking to understand
What voice might speak from stone

And though I never heard
For all its giant brooding
More than the silent word
Of old stone saying nothing,

That touch of lichen and granite
Silver and rough replying
Seemed word enough for the moment
And deeply satisfying.

SPEAKING OF WOMBATS

Once on a mountain
I was alone
In miles of moonlight
And granite stone.

Maybe the moon
Though far enough from us
Kept like a buttercup
Summer's soft promise,

But down the cold gorges
The river ran lost
Like ice and like iron
Through tussocks like frost

And the high crests rolled
So bright and so far
They made the earth seem
Remote as a star.

But speaking of wombats
One must assume
The higher the harder
The more they're at home

For there was this creature
Shambling and hairy
Lit by the moon
Like some wild furry fairy;

And for one moment
As if to prove
Granite and tussock
Could breathe and move

In the frost-smoke wreathing
Dark and uncertain
He stood by the river
And warmed the mountain;

Then somewhere he vanished
Where wombats go
Wandering in buttercups
Burrowing in snow

And in his high country
I was alone
In miles of moonlight
And granite stone.

THE WARATAHS

Then when he broke
Through the wall like glass
A hundred waratahs
Watched him trespass.

It was no place
To come to at will;
The wild bush lived there
Private and still.

If it was in time
It was different from ours,
If it was on earth
It belonged to wild flowers.

Honeyflower and heath
And small yellow pea
Gathered together
By the blackbutt tree

And the tall slim waratahs
So many and so many
Glimmered over all
Proud and uncanny.

Crimson they floated
To his left to his right
Like slow fiery suns
In the forest's green night.

But they were so still
And so tall and so silent
They looked like people
And he was half frightened.

It was so queer
To see them all stand
Crowned with red flame
In their own green land.

"The crow flies over
On its black loud wings
And I think that I tread in
The country of kings."

A SONNET ABOUT POSSUMS

Possums like poets somehow survive precariously
In city parks, even in holy St Mary's.
At night in suburban gardens they move mysteriously
Nibbling the rosebuds, flying in the moon like fairies.
Sometimes they carry on their backs their tiny progeny.
How can they survive when all other creatures of the wild,
Koala and wallaby, echidna and aborigine,
Have fled before us utterly unreconciled?

Their art is to seem to conform; to sit up nicely
When kindly housewives feed them on bread and sugar,
But never to be located quite precisely.
They know a midnight starrier than ours and huger
And there up gum-trees or wickedly lurking in ceilings
They slink and exult in their true wild animal feelings.

MEMORIES OF A VETERAN

Here comes an old soldier from World War One,
He fought not at Ypres, he was far from Verdun,
But he won the last battle (oh do break it down).

Then spare him a copper or buy him a beer
For he fought a lone fight (break it down) without fear
And when the war started his age was one year.

Three uncles I had, their name was FitzGerald,
They sailed off for France with their lives sore imperilled
To fight with the Kaiser with whom they had quarrelled.

Good luck to you then, Roy, Gerald, and Maurice,
Away where the nations were fighting like furies,
No doubt you did well but I've my own stories.

I recall (break it down) when I was a boy
Who played with a popgun and thought it a toy
The Germans took prisoner my bold uncle Roy.

But the war was far off from fair Eltham, New Zealand,
So I played by the creek with my friend Seymour Haden
And little we dreamed what the future kept hidden.

And Roy had a mind to fight on for his country,
He tunnelled for miles and when checked by a sentry
He calmly rode out in a truck-load of laundry.

On charged the brave British, the Germans were reeling,
At last it was won and the church bells were pealing
And great was the joy then in Eltham, New Zealand.

The Town Band was playing, the kilties were swinging,
The fire-bell as well as the church bells were ringing,
The whistles were blowing, men shouting and singing;

The Kaiser, alas just a dummy of course,
Was dragged through the town in Sam Pepperill's hearse,
The *Argus* was filled with bad prose and worse verse,

Such banners, such cheering, such blowing of bugles,
And up to the Park now the crowd seethes and struggles
And proudly amongst them march Seymour and Douglas.

And high on a plank in the Park stood the Mayor,
And the local M.P. and the parsons were there
All up on the platform world peace to declare.

Here comes an old soldier, I said so before,
And mine be the first drop of ale that you pour
For I won the last fight in the war to end war.

For young Seymour in spite or some awful mishap
(Break it down, break it down, there's no chance of escape)
Knocked off and tramped on my field-marshal's cap.

At Eltham on Peace Day began this great fight,
For Douglas hit Seymour, it seemed only right,
And Seymour hit Doug on the nose where it hurt.

And away from the Mayor in the midst of his speech
The people came rushing like waves on the beach,
They formed in a ring and they roared at each punch.

And Douglas hit Seymour and Seymour hit Douggie
On the nose (break it down), on the ribs, in the belly,
Till Seymour was winded and Douglas was groggy.

Oh I fear that our heroes weren't fitted for war,
They met not in rapture in battle's first jar
But circled each other in fear from afar,

But the crowd hemmed them in with its roars and its cheers,
They had to fight on, it seemed for four years,
Till Seymour was bleeding and Doug was in tears.

So here's an old soldier and long may he thrive,
He fought a great fight and he came back alive
To be cheered by all Eltham, a victor, aged five.

He's not one to fight now, he's not one to quarrel,
So spare him a copper and tip up the barrel,
And at least (break it down) he'll not point you the moral.

ELEGY

Oh I see clearly since cats and crocodiles and mice
Will never stop breeding because it is natural and nice
We must submit to death however it may hurt
Because it was half of the bargain from the start.

I do submit then, I acknowledge death is sensible,
Only it bites me and I feel it reprehensible;
The world is too crowded and death does trim it neatly
But I have been too much surrounded by it lately.

I mourn for my black-furred she-cat, and my father and my mother
And my aunt and my fierce proud uncle, if there isn't any other
Just now to lament, I dread what may lie in store
And I pray that death won't occur on the earth any more.

Take Mrs Tiddles now. Tiddles was my cat
And a mother of sixty kittens in five years flat;
But a kind cat, Tiddles, a soft cat, knew her station,
And was killed today by a bloody great Alsatian.

Take Eileen FitzGerald now, she was my aunt,
About the size of a peanut, whom nothing could daunt;
At the age of eighty wanted to fly a helicopter
And would have, too, only a heart attack stopped her.

Take Gerald FitzGerald who fought in the first world war
Where the black trenches cut across France like a scar
And, wounded somewhere, never stopped fighting after
But shook sometimes with a witty, bitter laughter.

Take, since he's taken indeed, Alec Stewart my father
Whom we dropped in his grave beside the blue sea water.
There in his green hill, far far away he lies
And stares through the earth at the sea with his big brown eyes.

Take Mary Stewart, who was Mary FitzGerald my mother,
And lie on her gently cold Eltham earth and weather;
So young she went, and so much gaiety in her—
But I'll not speak when grief's too deep to utter.

Oh they all live, perhaps, cats, parents and aunt,
Somewhere in shining heaven, but maybe they don't;
The cat is her kittens, and only poor souls in me
My father walks and my mother's blue eyes see.

I weep for what is no more, the strong personality,
The person walking the world in all its vitality;
I mourn for those who mean nothing to anybody
But once were the pillars of the earth and held me so steady.

True, I have seen old bones like a stone or a daisy
Cows' bones, sheep's bones, lying in the sun so easy,
And men's bones too, and I know that old death is nothing,
It is only the immediate that hurts, when the live thing stops
    breathing.

But these stood so close to me once and these are so recent,
My cat and my aunt are gone, and it is not decent.
I had not thought they were crowding the earth so thickly.
Oh earth, oh sun, oh rain, clean their bones quickly,

So once again but not with so much hurt
I may admit what I know for the truth in my heart,
Life was the half we had and the fine lovely part
But death was the rest of the bargain right from the start.

ARTHUR STACE

That shy mysterious poet Arthur Stace
Whose work was just one single mighty word
Walked in the utmost depths of time and space
And there his word was spoken and he heard.
Eternity, Eternity, it banged him like a bell
Dulcet from heaven sounding, sombre from hell.

Sometimes it twinkled to him in the sand
As though God winked at him, and then he smiled
And scooped it up to sift it through his hand;
Sometimes it roared upon him vast and wild
When the green seas rolled heaving from the Gap;
Appalled he stood, to think a man might leap

And swim those waves, and could if he had strength,
Could count the sand, if he had time enough,
And yet the sea was not one inch in length
Against those endless miles his thought slid off,
And though you counted the sand-grains ten times over
You'd not begun Eternity's awful number.

One two three four, sometimes he counted all day,
Five six seven eight, and on far into the night
By tens, by thousands, hoping to reach half way,
And still before his eyes like swans in flight
Though he got up to billions and to trillions
The numbers streamed away into the silence.

O it was in the sky that had no end
Where fiery worlds hung glittering in the void;
He thought of Heaven where man had his big friend
And that was safe he knew and that was good,
But at the back of heaven he felt, he feared,
The hellish dark ran on, the wild eyes glared.

And it was here in Monday, Tuesday, Friday,
In yesterday, tomorrow, morrow, morrow,
In Caesar's day, thought Arthur Stace, and my day;
It moved in him, it struck him deep with sorrow
That men should live in time with all its vanity
Or think they did, and yet were in Eternity.

For it was like a dark wind in their hair,
It burnt their eyes, it roared in their dull ears,
It flowed between their fingers with the air.
How could they be obsessed with worldly cares,
How could they sin, how waste one precious minute
When every step they took plunged deeper in it?

This must be told, he knew. But how to do it?
He was a quiet man and he was shy
And had no gift to speak, but like a poet
Must write the word that reached him from on high.
Eternity he'd heard great preachers shout
And shook to hear, but say it he could not.

No, it must come like moonlight or like frost
Silent at night like mushrooms quietly growing
To wake the wicked and redeem the lost;
Like a white feather in the dawn wind blowing,
Perfect and white, like copperplate in chalk;
And that was when Arthur Stace began to walk.

All night he walked and most nights of the week,
Treading with silent steps the silent town
Where none but drunks and whores were still awake,
His great word burning where he wrote it down;
Eternity he wrote, clear pure and pale
And underlined it with the y's long tail.

No night-bird saw him for he was an angel
Or almost that, upon his holy mission;
Unseen he passed the copper with his cudgel,
Unseen he climbed the steps at Town Hall station,
Invisible, like ectoplasm, he swam
Where shops were empty and where lights were dim.

Sometimes when midnight chimed in Martin Place
Behind the arches of the G.P.O.
A shadow moved, but was it Arthur Stace?
Some flickering thing perhaps crept soft and low
On the dark pavement by the Opera House
But was it hands that moved there or a mouse?

No one could say, one only knew for certain
That here, that there, in unexpected places
Somewhere that night the great word had been written
And Arthur Stace once more had left his traces
And bright and spry now like a leprechaun
Was stepping home to Pyrmont in the dawn.

Eternity, it fades like morning dew,
Like morning dew and he is lost in it;
Yet one can say, as one can say of few,
It was the greatest of all words he wrote
And if it hardly changed this wicked city
God rest his soul, his copperplate was pretty.

THE TAILOR FISHERMEN

In the winter dusk when the sea turns green and silver
And dazzling white as the tall wave topples in foam,
That is the time to fish from the beach for tailor
And over the sandhills the tailor fishermen come.

They know that this is a fish like the sea itself
With the same cool colours, the same white rushing intensity,
And they cast far out between a wave and a wave
Well pleased if they can be hooked to such an immensity.

And if there is nothing yet to snatch up the bait
Of garfish or mullet and pull like a horse in the breakers,
Well, they know how to fish so they know how to wait;
And while they are waiting I study these tailor takers.

And they look well with the gulls in the winter weather
With rain coming up and the wind on the long wet beach;
They stand in a fine democracy together
Each keeping his place and nobody talking too much;

They do not inquire each other's name and address,
Income, religion, status or nationality;
They accept each other by the long white foaming seas
As men who fish, and that is their rank and quality.

They acknowledge as a kind of kindred, old distant relations,
All salty objects cast up and dried in the sun,
The starfish lost from its far red constellations,
Cunjevoi, beadweed, sponge, white cuttlefish bone.

They nod with respect to the portuguese man-o'-war
Wet on the sand with its streamers like purple string;
They know it is what the sea is and what men are,
The deep blue heavenly bubble, the searing sting.

And they themselves as the dusk begins to deepen
Seem like some natural growth of the foam-wet sand;
Sombre and solitary, waiting for a fish to happen,
With the waves about them, like pillars of rock they stand.

And talking to no one, fishing in my own station,
I am glad to have stood with such people in the cold wind;
They haven't gone soft with too much civilization,
They practise an art that has been of use to mankind

And may be again in the wild white rolling of time;
And well that they should, for how the waves glint and roar
In the hollow of night when they pack their gear and go home
And no one is fishing for tailor any more.

FOR KENNETH SLESSOR

Hang it all, Slessor, as Pound once said to Browning,
Why have you sailed so untimely out on the water
To vanish up in a cloud or down by drowning
Whichever it was? You should have died hereafter.

For though you've left your verse to make amends
And so it does, as much as verse can do,
You were a man who liked to meet his friends
And here we are but where in the world are you?

Still at the top of your stairs I see you stand
Bowing a little in your courtly manner,
Smiling and gracious, shining and pink and rotund,
Bidding us into the privilege of your dinner.

And in your dining room that you've made noble
With walls of books that climb up shelf by shelf
From floor to ceiling, there's your dark wood table
Gleaming with silver you've laid out yourself,

For men must eat their beef in decent splendour
Wherever their wives and mistresses have flown
And since those bright mad girls had all gone under
The ocean somewhere, superbly you cooked your own.

I think of how we sat there light and lucky
While the soft candlelight flowed round the room
And heard you talk of Pepys and William Hickey,
Tennyson's verse and drunken pranks of Lamb;

Or venturing forth, where oystery rocks were waiting
At Bobbin Head and you were Captain Slessor,
Staunch on your launch I see you navigating
Like Captain Dobbin, your great predecessor,

And can't believe you've sunk; yet sunk you have,
Or flown or gone, and so with due apology
I raise my voice in necessary grief
And trespass in your private field of elegy.

And yet the day you died when I went walking
—Where else to go?—restless to Circular Quay
There had come in a tide so huge and sparkling
It filled all Sydney with the open sea,

And while it flowed from Manly to Balmain
With seagulls white on it, the great blue tide,
And washed the harbour sparkling clean again
As though no man had ever drowned or died,

I thought how with your spacious hospitality
In its high tide you'd made all life a feast;
And how your verse in its rich lustrous quality
Flowed round us still though you were far and lost,

And suddenly knew it still was good that morning,
Whatever else might happen in the world,
To see that noble tide now full and turning;
And in my grief I was half reconciled.

Well, round and ripe and rich with years you went
As if you rode that great tide out to sea
And we salute you even as we lament
And drink your health wherever you may be.

BELL ROCK

So in the sea's long sparkle of blue and silver
Back to the shore came Stevenson, and thought:
There then, it's done, and may no wave knock it over
For out of all fear, all thunder, confusion and doubt
One thing is accomplished, aye, to the best of my power,
And there in the wind's teeth I have built my tower.

And built it, too, so now in my mind it seems,
Out of foam and wave-tops, cries of the gulls in the wind,
Snatches of storm and sunlight, like a tower of dreams;
For how except in some fairyland of the mind
Could man have built it where no tower could be
Standing and flashing out in the naked sea?

Aye it is rooted in rock and made with hands
And yet in the nights like nightmare there I woke
On the tossing ship in the moonlight's iron bands
And saw as the water fell old black Bell Rock
Heave out like the world's beginning, and stared appalled
To think it was there we must stand, there we must build.

Yet there in the black disaster in the great gale
On that incredible night of struggle and slaughter,
Lost in the darkness, the fleet of seventy sail,
Ship after ship had struck and perished in the water,
Frigate and cutter, the tall proud *Duke of York*
With all their sailors drowning around Bell Rock.

Once there had been a bell that the abbot hung
And the pirate stole, so the old story ran:
And truth or fable, this had lain wait too long
Against the pride and the purposes of man.
No ship could pass on the coast or sail from Tay
But stark or hidden in its path the monster lay.

So then you damned old killer, prickly with barnacles,
Slippery with bright green weed in the morning sun,
In twisted iron in your crevices we read your chronicles
Of broken ships and seamen doomed to drown
And while the foam raced off you flower by flower
So white, so cold, knew we must build our tower.

243

And so at each low tide, two hours to work
Before the water was splashing about our knees,
In summer sunlight, out of the ocean's dark
Far on Bell Rock amongst the crashing of the seas
We saw the white birds wheel, the porpoise leap,
And stone upon stone we built our lighthouse up.

But not like that, not stone by stone at ease
Brought out by dancing lighters on the tide
And rowed ashore and neatly dropped in place
And no one tumbling headlong in the weed.
There's no man built a tower upon the water
But met his share of terror and disaster.

They said no man could build upon Bell Rock
And so thought I, and many times I doubted,
Fearing to start, fearing the years of work,
And most of all, as each long night we waited,
And paced the deck and peered through fog and spray,
Fearing the tide had washed our work away.

And there was human stubbornness forbye
That wants its rights at inconvenient seasons
Though the work lags and there the rock lies dry.
The stones were laid, ye ken, by Tay-side masons,
Good honest brave mad Presbyterian folk
Who would not work on Sundays—at Bell Rock!

Blood of my blood, faith of my faith, ye rascals,
Then pray on the Sabbath, pray each day of the week
When winter comes and man must leave his castles,
Even his half-done tower upon Bell Rock,
That wind and wave may spare the work of his hands,
Not sweep it away like a child's game on the sands.

Aye, and it stood, all stained with spray and slime,
And the boat that black fine morning overturned
And young Alec Scott was snatched away to his doom
And terribly in the tide his white face burned
Now clear, now lost, now clear, further and further
Until there was only sky to see, and the rock and the water.

Oh but I thought to lose one dreadful night
Men, tower, my work, my worthless self, my all;
For the tide rose, and the mist, and we waited for the boat
And the tide rose, and no boat came to our call;
And I turned to my men to say some words of cheer
And could not speak, I was so dry with fear.

And wearily, wearily, flew the storm's white shower,
Wearily, wearily tossed our little ship,
Wearily, scarily, crouched our men in the tower
As still with pain and labour the work took shape;
Till one bright evening it was done at last,
Whatever the toil had been, whatever the cost.

Aye, it was done, and I'll not be too proud
But give to God the credit and my masons
And think of great cathedrals like a cloud
Shining with lightning, filling whole horizons.
Here's just one stubborn Scottish engineer
Who piled up stones to make a light shine clear.

Yet there it stood, tall golden tower and lamp
Bare at low tide, deep in the water at high,
And the sea welled up and flung its spray to the top
And it stood trembling a little in the water and sky
When the big waves battered against it, uncanny to feel,
Uneasy, uncanny, and yet it did not fall.

Winter for it, and the safe shore for me
In silver light, nor fear the looming thunder;
Yet I have built my tower in the deep sea
Which men may note perhaps with some small wonder;
And while it stands, as stand it will with luck,
There shall be no more shipwrecks on Bell Rock.

The History of Colour

K. F. PEARSON

She is complete
and in her beauty's complete.

That which is outside her face's beauty
is less than the sum of beauty.

Above all a resourceful shape-shifter, the South Australian poet K. F. Pearson keeps trying, and succeeding with, different modes and pitches of poetry. From imitations of Polynesian chant and Arctic ghazal to a delicious satire on applying for funding, from autobiographical sketches to highly worked portraits, and equally in richly rewarding examples of that intense meditation on particulars which tests a good poet by being so well-worked a field, Pearson displays a versatility and a freshness well worthy of the abundant life in his chosen topics.

Orpheus

A. D. HOPE

As he approaches the end of a distinguished career, the elder statesman of Australian poetry is writing as well as ever. Yet even the most fervent of A. D. Hope's admirers will be astonished by the range and power of this latest collection of his work, which is published in his 85th year.

Though several of these poems face the sad truth of bodily disintegration, they do so cheerfully, with ironic wit rather than with morbidity. Other poems deal just as wittily with Hope's familiar theme of carnal love, most notably in the rollicking bawdy ballad 'Teaser rams'.

The sequence 'Western Elegies', at the beginning of the book, touches on all of Hope's major concerns — love and language and mortality — and is moreover a revolutionary technical departure. It is the work of a master, still at the height of his powers.

Singing the Snake

BILLY MARSHALL-STONEKING

Billy has lived among our people and has taken the time to understand us. If there were more people like him, Australia would be a much better place for all Koori people. His poems mean a great deal to me.

Ruby Langford, Author of DON'T TAKE YOUR LOVE TO TOWN

One of Billy Marshall-Stoneking's great strengths is that he is very sensitive to the mystery between his own culture and that of his Aboriginal friends. The long, hard years of being with the Papunya people have been illuminated by this sensitivity...

Barrett Reid, Poet and Editor of OVERLAND

A teller of wonderful stories who made me know my shame—and my laughter.

Terry Gilmore, Poet

Collected Poems

ROSEMARY DOBSON

Rosemary Dobson's *Collected Poems* brings together almost two hundred poems written over a period of fifty years. The book will be one of the abiding joys of Australian literature, a lifework of love and dedication to the craft of writing. It presents the poet's work as a whole and shows the progress and the diversity of her art, so often characterised by wit and irony.

Many of the poems are close to epistles or letters. They belong to this world, its people and events. They surprise, however, with their weight of feeling and nervous insight, and with what James McAuley wrote of as this poet's 'sense of a mystery . . . momentarily glimpsed'.

Rosemary Dobson's style with its spare, clean and hard qualities is European in its emphases. Yet she has been subtle and sensitive in her awareness of Australia as her place of belonging. She has shared with Judith Wright, A. D. Hope, James McAuley, David Campbell and Les Murray a pre-eminence among modern Australian poets. Her strong recent development in the 1980s and her perseverance as an artist reveal a classical sense of tradition that is open to change and the future.

Confessions of a Corinthian

JULIAN CROFT

The name of ancient Corinth was for centuries a synonym for luxury and self-indulgence. By rebelling against what he saw as a paralysed and parochial Australia of his youth, the poet Julian Croft now considers that he helped to create a pervasive Corinth in Australia, one in which the slow erosion of values in the small towns of our east coast horrifies him as much as the excesses of Surfers Paradise. In coming to terms with how we create consciousness, and his part in creating a crummy one, he explores the past in Proustian detail, and examines the latest insights of a human-centred theory of physics. The poetry in which he deals with all of these concerns maintains the verve and feeling familiar from his celebrated earlier collection *Breakfast in Shanghai*.